1st Workshop on Predicting and Improving Text Readability for Target Reader Populations 2012

Held at the 2012 Conference of the North American Chapter of the Association for Computational Linguistics: Human Language Technologies (NAACL-HLT 2012)

Montreal, Quebec, Canada
3-8 June 2012

ISBN: 978-1-62276-550-8

Printed from e-media with permission by:

Curran Associates, Inc.
57 Morehouse Lane
Red Hook, NY 12571

Some format issues inherent in the e-media version may also appear in this print version.

Printed by Curran Associates, Inc. (2013)

For permission requests, please contact the Association for Computational Linguistics at the address below.

Association for Computational Linguistics
209 N. Eighth Street
Stroudsburg, Pennsylvania 18360

Phone: 1-570-476-8006
Fax: 1-570-476-0860

acl@aclweb.org

Additional copies of this publication are available from:

Curran Associates, Inc.
57 Morehouse Lane
Red Hook, NY 12571 USA
Phone: 845-758-0400
Fax: 845-758-2634
Email: curran@proceedings.com
Web: www.proceedings.com

Foreword

The last few years have seen a resurgence of work on text simplification and readability. Examples include learning lexical and syntactic simplification operations from Simple English Wikipedia revision histories, exploring more complex lexico-syntactic simplification operations requiring morphological changes as well as constituent reordering, simplifying mathematical form, applications for target users such as deaf students, second language learners and low literacy adults, and fresh attempts at predicting readability.

The PITR 2012 workshop has been organised to provide a cross-disciplinary forum for discussing key issues related to predicting and improving text readability for target users. It will be held on June 7, 2012 in conjunction with the 2012 Conference of the North American Chapter of the Association for Computational Linguistics: Human Language Technologies, in Montréal, Québec, and is sponsored by the ACL Special Interest Group on Speech and Language Processing for Assistive Technologies (SIG-SLPAT).

These proceedings include eight papers that cover various perspectives on the topic, from machine learning to psycholinguistic methods. Three papers try to distinguish between surface level fluency and deeper comprehensibility issues (Rello et al.; Siddharthan and Katsos; Maney et al.). Other papers focus on feature engineering for better predicting and interpreting readability (Francois and Miltsakaki; Tonelli et al; Ma et al). Two papers specifically address the issue of lexical difficulty (Drndarevic and Saggion; Brooke et al).

We hope this volume is a valuable addition to the literature, and look forward to an exciting Workshop.

Sandra Williams
Advaith Siddharthan
Ani Nenkova

Organizers:

Sandra Williams, The Open University, UK.
Advaith Siddharthan, University of Aberdeen, UK.
Ani Nenkova, University of Pennsylvania, USA.

Program Committee:

Gregory Aist, Iowa State University, USA.
John Carroll, University of Sussex, UK.
Kevyn Collins-Thompson, Microsoft Research (Redmond), USA.
Siobhan Devlin, University of Sunderland, UK.
Noémie Elhadad, Columbia University, USA.
Micha Elsner, University of Edinburgh, UK.
Richard Evans, University of Wolverhampton, UK.
Lijun Feng, Columbia University, USA.
Caroline Gasperin, TouchType Ltd., UK.
Albert Gatt, University of Malta, Malta.
Pablo Gervás, Universidad Complutense de Madrid, Spain.
Iryna Gurevych, Technische Universitat Darmstadt, Germany.
Raquel Hervás, Universidad Complutense de Madrid, Spain.
Véronique Hoste, University College Ghent, Belgium.
Matt Huenerfauth, The City University of New York (CUNY), USA.
Iustina Ilisei, University of Wolverhampton, UK.
Tapas Kanungo, Microsoft, USA.
Mirella Lapata, University of Edinburgh, UK.
Annie Louis, University of Pennsylvania, USA.
Ruslan Mitkov, University of Wolverhampton, UK.
Hitoshi Nishikawa, NTT, Japan.
Mari Ostendorf, University of Washington, USA.
Ehud Reiter, University of Aberdeen, UK.
Lucia Specia, University of Wolverhampton, UK.
Irina Temnikova, University of Wolverhampton, UK.
Ielka van der Sluis, University of Groningen, The Netherlands.

Invited Talk: *Enriching the Web with Readability Metadata*

Dr Kevyn Collins-Thompson, Microsoft Research, USA.

Table of Contents

Workshop Program

Thursday, June 7, 2012

Invited Talk

9:15–9:30 Opening Remarks

9:30–10:30 Invited Talk by Kevyn Collins-Thompson: Enriching the Web with Readability Metadata

Coffee

Session 1: What is readability

11:00–11:15 *Toward Determining the Comprehensibility of Machine Translations*
Tucker Maney, Linda Sibert, Dennis Perzanowski, Kalyan Gupta and Astrid Schmidt-Nielsen

11:15–11:30 *Towards Automatic Lexical Simplification in Spanish: An Empirical Study*
Biljana Drndarevic and Horacio Saggion

11:30–11:45 *Offline Sentence Processing Measures for testing Readability with Users*
Advaith Siddharthan and Napoleon Katsos

11:45–12:00 *Graphical Schemes May Improve Readability but Not Understandability for People with Dyslexia*
Luz Rello, Horacio Saggion, Ricardo Baeza-Yates and Eduardo Graells

12.00–12:30 Panel Discussion

Thursday, June 7, 2012 (continued)

Lunch

Session 2: Predicting readability

14:00–14:15 *Building Readability Lexicons with Unannotated Corpora*
Julian Brooke, Vivian Tsang, David Jacob, Fraser Shein and Graeme Hirst

14:15–14:30 *Making Readability Indices Readable*
Sara Tonelli, Ke Tran Manh and Emanuele Pianta

14:30–14:45 *Do NLP and machine learning improve traditional readability formulas?*
Thomas François and Eleni Miltsakaki

14:45–15:00 *Comparing human versus automatic feature extraction for fine-grained elementary readability assessment*
Yi Ma, Ritu Singh, Eric Fosler-Lussier and Robert Lofthus

\+ 15:00–15:30 Panel Discussion

Poster Session

15:30–17:30 Coffee + Joint Poster Session with SLPAT

Business Meeting

17:30–18:30 SIG-SLPAT Business Meeting

Toward Determining the Comprehensibility of Machine Translations

Tucker Maney, Linda Sibert, and Dennis Perzanowski
Naval Research Laboratory
4555 Overlook Avenue, SW
Washington, DC
{tucker.maney|linda.sibert|dennis.perzanowski}@nrl.navy.mil

Kalyan Gupta and Astrid Schmidt-Nielsen
Knexus Research Corporation
163 Waterfront Street, Suite 440
National Harbor, MD
{kalyan.gupta.ctr|astrid.schmidtnielsen.ctr}@nrl.navy.mil

Abstract

Economic globalization and the needs of the intelligence community have brought machine translation into the forefront. There are not enough skilled human translators to meet the growing demand for high quality translations or "good enough" translations that suffice only to enable understanding. Much research has been done in creating translation systems to aid human translators and to evaluate the output of these systems. Metrics for the latter have primarily focused on improving the overall quality of entire test sets but not on gauging the understanding of individual sentences or paragraphs. Therefore, we have focused on developing a theory of translation effectiveness by isolating a set of translation variables and measuring their effects on the comprehension of translations. In the following study, we focus on investigating how certain linguistic permutations, omissions, and insertions affect the understanding of translated texts.

1. Introduction

There are numerous methods for measuring translation quality and ongoing research to improve relevant and informative metrics (see http://www.itl.nist.gov/iad/mig/tests/metricsmatr) (Przybocki et al., 2008). Many of these automated metrics, including BLEU and NIST, were created to be used only for aggregate counts over an entire test-set. The effectiveness of these methods on translations of short segments remains unclear (Kulesza and Shieber, 2004). Moreover, most of these tools are useful for comparing different systems, but do not attempt to identify the most dominant cause of errors. All errors are not equal and as such should be evaluated depending on their consequences (Schiaffino and Zearo, 2005).

Recently, researchers have begun looking at the frequencies of errors in translations of specific language pairs. Vilar et al. (2006) presented a typology for annotating errors and used it to classify errors between Spanish and English and from Chinese into English. Popovic and Ney (2011) used methods for computing Word Error Rate (WER) and Position-independent word Error Rate (PER) to outline a procedure for automatic error analysis and classification. They evaluated their methodology by looking at translations into English from Arabic, Chinese and German and two-way English-Spanish data (Popovic and Ney, 2007). Condon et al. (2010) used the US National Institute of Standards and Technology's NIST post-editing tool to annotate errors in English-Arabic translations

These methods have all focused on finding frequencies of individual error categories, not on determining their effect on comprehension. In machine translation environments where post-editing is used to produce the same linguistic quality as would be achieved by standard human translation, such a focus is justified. A greater reduction in the time needed to correct a translation would be achieved by eliminating errors that frequently occur.

However, there are situations in which any translation is an acceptable alternative to no translation, and the direct (not post-edited) content is given to the user. Friends chatting via instant messaging tools or reading foreign-language e-mail mainly want to understand roughly what is being said. When a Marine is out patrolling and needs to interact with the local inhabitants to get information, it is "far better to have a machine [translation] than to not have anything" (Gallafent, 2011). For such purposes, automated translation can provide a "gist" of the meaning of the original message as long as it is comprehensible. In such situations, errors that affect comprehension trump those that occur frequently and should receive a greater focus in efforts to improve output quality.

Recently, companies have begun customizing translation engines for use in specific environments. IBM and Lionbridge's GeoFluent (http://en-us.lionbridge.com/GeoFluent/GeoFluent.htm) uses customization to improve translation output for online chatting and other situations where post-editing is not feasible. TranSys (http://www.multicorpora.com/en/products/product-options-and-add-ons/multitrans-prism-transys/) from Mutlicorpora and Systran also uses customization to deliver translations ready for immediate distribution or for human post-editing. Knowing the major factors for creating understandable text can play a role in perfecting such systems.

Research has not settled on a single methodology for classifying translation errors. Two of the five categories proposed by Vilar et al. (2006), missing words and word order, are the focus of this project. Missing word errors fall into two categories, those essential to the meaning of the sentence and those only necessary for grammatical correctness. Only the first of these is addressed here. Likewise, there is a distinction between word- or phrase-based reordering. The results of the experiment presented in this paper are concerned only with the latter.

The present research seeks to determine the impact of specific error types on comprehension. We contend that research efforts should focus on those errors resulting in misinterpretation, not just on those that occur most often. This project therefore focuses on the use of linguistic parameters, including omissions and changes in word order, to determine the effect on comprehensibility of machine translations at the sentence and paragraph level.

2. Methodology

The first step in this research was determining the linguistic parameters to be investigated. Nine sentence types exhibiting the following characteristics were selected:

- Deleted verb
- Deleted adjective
- Deleted noun
- Deleted pronoun
- Modified prepositions *in*, *on*, *at* to an alternate one (e.g. *in* → *at*)
- Modified word order to SOV (Subject, Object, Verb)
- Modified word order to VOS
- Modified word order to VSO
- Retained SVO word order (control).

The one additional parameter, modifying a preposition, was added to the original list because it is a frequent error of translations into English (Takahaski, 1969).

The next step was to identify a means to test comprehension. Sachs (1967) contends that a sentence has been understood if it is represented in one's memory in a form that preserves its meaning, but not necessarily its surface structure. Royer's (Royer et al., 1987) Sentence Verification Technique (SVT) is a technique for measuring the comprehension of text paragraphs by determining if such a representation has been created. It has been used for three decades and been shown to be a reliable and valid technique for measuring comprehension in a wide variety of applications (Pichette et al., 2009).

In composing SVT tests, several paragraphs, each containing approximately 12 sentences, are chosen. For each of the sentences appearing in the original text, four test sentences are created. One is an exact copy of the original sentence and another, a paraphrase of that sentence. A "meaning change" test sentence is one in which a few words are changed in order to alter the meaning of the sentence. The fourth test sentence is a "distractor" which is consistent with the text of the original, but is not related in meaning to any sentence in the original passage (Royer et al., 1979).

We used a similar measure, a variation of the Meaning Identification Technique (MIT) (Marchant et al., 1988), a simpler version of the test that was developed out of the SVT and corrected for some of its shortfalls. Here, there are only two test sentence types presented, either a paraphrase of the original sentence or a "meaning change" sentence. In the description of the MIT technique for sentence creation, a paraphrase is created for each sentence in the original text and altering this paraphrase produces the "meaning change" sentence. In this experiment, the original sentence, not the paraphrase, was used to produce a sentence using many of the same words but with altered meaning.

In the test, readers are asked to read a passage, in our case a passage in which the linguistic parameters have been manipulated in a controlled fashion (see Section 3 (2)). Then with the text no longer visible, they are presented with a series of syntactically correct sentences shown one at a time in random order and asked to label them as being "old" or "new", relative to the passage they have just read (see Section 3 (3)). A sentence should be marked "old" if it has the same meaning as a sentence in the original paragraph and "new" otherwise. "New" sentences contain information that was absent from or contradictory to that in the original passage.

3. Experiment

The first requirement of the study was developing paragraphs to be used for the experiment. Eleven passages found on the WEB, many of which were GLOSS (http://gloss.dliflc.edu/search.aspx) online language lessons, were edited to consist of exactly nine sentences. These paragraphs, containing what will be referred to as the original sentences, served as the basis for building the passages to be read by the participants and for creating the sentences to be used in the test.

The next step was to apply the linguistic parameters under study to create the paragraphs to be read initially by the reader. One of the linguistic parameters listed above was randomly chosen and applied to alter a sentence within each paragraph, so that each paragraph contained exactly one of each of the parameter changes. However, pronouns and prepositions were not present in all sentences. When one of these was the parameter to be changed in a given sentence but was not present, adjustments had to be made in the original pairing of sentences with the other linguistic parameters. The changes were done as randomly as possible but in such a way that each paragraph still contained one of each type of parameter modification.

In sentences in which the change was an omission, the word to delete was chosen randomly from all those in the sentence having the same part of speech (POS). For sentences in which the preposition needed to be modified, the choice was randomly chosen from the two remaining alternatives as listed above in Section 2.

In creating the test sentences, the original sentences were again used. For each sentence within each paragraph, a committee of four, two of which were linguists, decided upon both a paraphrase and a meaning change sentence. Then, within each paragraph, the paraphrase of four randomly chosen sentences and the meaning change alternative for four others, also randomly picked, were selected. The ninth sentence randomly fell in either the paraphrase or meaning change category.

After reading the altered paragraph, the participant saw four or five sentences that were paraphrases of the original sentences and four or five sentences that were "meaning change" sentences, all in random order. The following is (1) an example of part of an original paragraph and (2) the same section linguistically altered. In (2), the alterations are specified in brackets after each sentence. Participants in the study did not, of course, see these identifiers. In (3), the sample comprehension questions posed after individuals read the linguistically altered passages are presented. In (3), the answers are provided in brackets after each sentence. Again, participants did not see the latter.

(1) World powers regard space explorations as the best strategy to enhance their status on the globe. Space projects with cutting-edge technologies not only serve as the best strategy to enhance their status on the globe. Korea must have strong policies to catch up with the space powers. The nation needs an overarching organization that manages all its space projects, similar to the National Aeronautics and Space Administration (NASA) and the European Space Agency (ESA). In addition, a national consensus must be formed if a massive budget is to be allocated with a long-term vision. Only under these

circumstances can the nation's brightest minds unleash their talent in the field.

(2) World powers regard space explorations as the best strategy to enhance status on the globe. [PRO] Space projects with cutting-edge technologies not only as the driver of growth in future industries and technological development, but play a pivotal role in military strategies. [VERB] Korea strong policies space powers the to catch up with have must. [SOV] Needs an overarching organization that manages all its space projects, similar to the National Aeronautics and Space Administration (NASA) and the European Space Agency (ESA) the nation. [VOS] In addition, a national consensus must be formed if a massive budget is to be allocated with a vision. [ADJ] Can unleash, only under these circumstances, the nation's brightest minds their talent in the field. [VSO]

(3) World powers regard space explorations as a viable, but expensive strategy to enhance their status among other countries. [NEW] Though space projects can be important for military purposes, the long-term costs can hamper a country's development in other areas. [NEW] To perform on a par with the predominate players in space exploration, Korea must develop robust policies. [OLD] Managing all of the nation's space projects will require a central organization, similar to the United States' National Aeronautics and Space Administration (NASA). [OLD] Securing the necessary budget and allocating these funds in accordance with a long-term vision will require national consensus. [OLD] The nation's brightest minds will be expected to work in the aerospace field. [NEW]

20 people volunteered as participants, consisting of 11 males and 9 females. All were over 25 years of age. All had at least some college, with 15 of the 20 holding advanced degrees. Only two did not list English as their native language. Of these, one originally spoke Polish, the other Farsi/Persian. Both had learned English by the age of 15 and considered themselves competent English speakers.

Participants were tested individually. Each participant was seated at a computer workstation equipped with a computer monitor, a keyboard and mouse. The display consisted of a series of screens displaying the passage, followed by the test sentences and response options.

At the start, participants completed two training passages. The paragraph read in the first had no linguistic alterations, while the second was representative of what the participants would see when doing the actual experiment. For both passages, after selecting a response option for a test sentence, the correct answer and reason for it was shown. There was an optional third training passage that no one elected to use.

During the experiment, participants were asked to read a passage. After finishing, with the text no longer in view, they were asked to rate a series of sentences as to whether they contained "old" or "new" information, relative to the information presented in the passage. Every participant viewed the same passages, but the order in which they were shown was randomized. Likewise, the sentences to be rated for a given passage were shown in varied order. Participants' keyboard interactions were time-stamped and their choices digitally recorded using software specifically designed for this experiment.

After completing the test session, participants were asked to complete a short online questionnaire. This was used to obtain background information, such as age, educational level, and their reactions during the experiment.

4. Software

The interface for the experiment and final questionnaire were developed using QuestSys, a web-based survey system that is part of the custom web application framework, Cobbler, licensed by Knexus Research Corporation. Cobbler is written in Python and uses the web framework CherryPy and the database engine SQLite, both from the public domain.

5. Results

During the test, participants choose either "old" or "new" after reading each sentence. The number they correctly identified out of the total viewed for that condition in all paragraphs was determined. This score, the proportion correct (pc) for each condition, is as follows:

SVO	0.788 (control)
PREP	0.854
PRO	0.800
SOV	0.790
NOUN	0.769
VOS	0.769
VSO	0.757
ADJ	0.689
VERB	0.688

The average performance for SVT is about 75% correct. In a valid test, one at the appropriate level for the population being tested, overall group averages should not fall below 65% or above 85% (Royer et al., 1987). The results of this experiment were consistent with these expectations.

Because pc does not take into account a person's bias for answering yes or no, it is considered to be a poor measure of one's ability to recognize a stimulus. This is because the response chosen in a discrimination task is known to be a product of the evidence for the presence of the stimulus and the bias of the participant to choose one response over the other. Signal Detection Theory (SDT) is frequently used to factor out bias when evaluating the results of tasks in which a person distinguishes between two different responses to a stimulus (Macmillan and Creelman, 1991). It has been applied in areas such as lie detection (truth/lie), inspection (acceptable /unacceptable), information retrieval (relevant /irrelevant) and memory experiments (old/new) (Stanislaw and Todorov, 1999). In the latter, participants are shown a list of words and subsequently asked to indicate whether or not they remember seeing a particular word. This experiment was similar: users were asked, not about remembering a "word", but to determine if they had read a sentence having the same meaning.

The unbiased proportion correct, $p(c)_{max}$, a metric provided by SDT was used to generate unbiased figures from the biased ones. For yes-no situations, such as this experiment,
$p(c)_{max} = \Phi\ (d'/2)$, where $d' = z\ (H) - z\ (F)$, H being the hit rate and F, the false alarm rate.

Larger d' values indicate that a participant sees a clearer difference between the "old" and "new" data. The d' values near zero demonstrate chance performance. Perfect performance results in an infinite d' value. To avoid getting infinite results, any 0 or 1 values obtained for an individual user were converted to 1/(2N) and 1-1/(2N) (Macmillan and Creelman, 1991). Negative values, which usually indicate response confusion, were eliminated.

The results of Single Factor Anova of $p(c)_{max}$ are shown below (Table 1). Since the F value exceeds the F-crit, the null hypothesis that all treatments were essentially equal must be rejected at the 0.05 level of significance.

Dunnett's t statistic (Winer et al., 1991) (Table 2) was used to determine if there was a significant difference between any of the eight sentence variations and the control (SVO). The results are given below.

The critical value for a one-tailed 0.05 test: $t_{0.95}$ (9,167) $\approx$ 2.40. The results in Table 2 indicate that, in this experiment, adjective (ADJ) and verb deletions (VERB) had a significant effect on the understanding of short paragraphs. Other deletions and changes in word order were not shown to significantly alter comprehension.

6. Discussion

Though translation errors vary by language pair and direction, this research focused on two areas that cause problems in translations into English: word deletion and alterations in word order. It looked at how these errors affect the comprehension of sentences contained in short paragraphs.

In the research cited above (Vilar et al. (2006), Condon et al. (2010), and Popovic and Ney (2007; 2011)), wrong lexical choice caused the most errors, followed by missing words. For the GALE corpora for Chinese and Arabic translations into English, Popovic and Ney (2011) categorized missing words by POS classes. The POS that predominated varied by language but verbs were consistently at the top, adjectives near the bottom. Our study showed that both significantly affect the comprehension of a paragraph. Deleted nouns, prepositions and pronouns did contribute to the overall error rate, but none proved important to the reader in interpreting the text. Word order modifications were not a major cause of errors in the research above, nor did they appear to cause problems in our experiment. These results lead us to argue that in situations where there may be no or limited post-editing, reducing errors in verb translation should be a

SUMMARY				
Groups	*Count*	*Sum*	*Average*	*Variance*
SVO	19	15.75532	0.829227	0.01104
PREP	20	17.12685	0.856343	0.017096
PRO	20	16.17873	0.808936	0.013273
SOV	20	16.24132	0.812066	0.0135
NOUN	20	16.04449	0.802225	0.010088
VOS	20	15.9539	0.797695	0.011276
VSO	19	15.13767	0.796719	0.020403
ADJ	19	13.78976	0.725777	0.010103
VERB	19	13.88158	0.730609	0.015428

ANOVA						
Source of Variation	*SS*	*df*	*MS*	*F*	*P-value*	*F crit*
Between Groups	0.27809	8	0.034761	2.563014	0.011608	1.994219813
Within Groups	2.264963	167	0.013563			
Total	2.543053	175				

Table 1. Anova Single Factor of $p(c)_{max}$

PREP	PRO	SOV	NOUN	VOS	VSO	ADJ	VERB
0.736215	-0.55093	-0.46596	-0.73316	-0.85615	-0.86029	-2.7377	-2.60981

Table 2. Dunnett's t statistic

major focus in machine translation research. Though missing adjectives also significantly affected comprehension, a commitment of resources to solve an infrequently occurring problem may be unwarranted. It must be noted, however, that the data used in reporting error frequencies was limited to Chinese and Arabic. Further research is still required to determine the applicability of these findings for translating from other languages into English.

7. Conclusion

In this experiment, the paragraph appears to have provided enough context for the reader to correctly surmise most missing words and to understand an altered word order. The deletion of an adjective or verb, however, caused a significant decline in comprehensibility. In research by others dealing with error frequencies, verbs were frequently missing in English translation output, adjectives rarely.

This suggests that translation of verbs should receive more attention as research in machine translation continues, particularly in systems designed to produce "good enough" translations.

This was a small test and the part of speech chosen for elimination was not necessarily the most salient. It is unknown if a longer test, involving more passages, or passages in which the missing word was always significant, would have amplified these results.

This study used the Sentence Verification Technique in a novel way. Though constructing the test requires some expertise, it provides a way to test the comprehensibly of translation output without the use of experienced translators or reference translations produced by such translators.

Acknowledgements

The authors would like to thank Rachael Richardson for her research contributions. The US Naval Research Laboratory supported this research through funding from the US Office of Naval Research.

References

Condon, Sherri, Dan Parvaz, John Aberdeen, Christy Doran, Andrew Freeman, and Marwan Awad. (2010). English and Iraqi Arabic. In *Proceedings of the Seventh International Conference on Language Resources and Evaluation (LREC'10),* Valletta, Malta, May 19-21.

Gallafent, Alex. (2011). Machine Translation for the Military. In *The World*, April 26, 2011.

Gamon, Michael, Anthony Aue, and Martine Smets. (2005). Sentence-level-MT evaluation without reference translations: Beyond language modeling. In *EAMT 2005 Conference Proceedings*, pp. 103-111, Budapest.

Kulesza, Alex and Stuart Shieber. (2004). A learning approach to improving sentence-level MT evaluation. In *Proceedings of the 10th International Conference on Theoretical and Methodological Issues in Machine Translation*, Baltimore, MD, October 4–6.

Lavie, Alon, Kenji Sagae, and Shyamsundar Jayaraman. (2004). The Significance of Recall in Automatic Metrics for MT Evaluation. In *Proceedings of the 6th Conference of the Association for Machine Translation in the Americas (AMTA-2004),* pp. 134–143. Washington, DC.

Macmillan, Neil and C. Douglas Creelman. (1991). Detection theory: A User's guide. Cambridge University Press, pp. 10 &125.

Marchant, Horace, James Royer and Barbara Greene. (1988). Superior reliability and validity for a new form of the Sentence Verification Technique for measuring comprehension. In *Educational and Psychological Measurement*, 48, pp. 827-834.

Pichette, François, Linda De Serres, and Marc Lafontaine. (2009). Measuring L2 reading comprehension ability using SVT tests. *Round Table Panels and Poster Presentation for the Language and Reading Comprehension for Immigrant Children (LARCIC),* May, 2009.

Popovic, Maja and Hermann Ney. (2007) Word Error Rates: Decomposition over POS Classes and Applications for Error Analysis. In *Proceeding of the Second Workshop on Statistical Machine Translation*, pp. 48-55, Prague.

Popovic, Maja and Hermann Ney. (2011) Towards Automatic Error Analysis of Machine Translation Output. *Computational Linguistics*, 37 (4): 657-688.

Przybocki, Mark, Kay Peterson, and Sébastien Bronsart. (2008). *Official results of the NIST 2008 "Metrics for MAchine TRanslation" Challenge (MetricsMATR08)*, http://nist.gov/speech/tests/metricsmatr/2008/results/

Royer, James, Barbara Greene, and Gale Sinatra. (1987). The Sentence Verification Technique: A practical procedure teachers can use to develop their own reading and listening comprehension tests. *Journal of Reading*, 30: 414-423.

Royer, James, Nicholas Hastings, and Colin Hook. (1979). A sentence verification technique for measuring reading comprehension. *Journal of Reading Behavior*, 11:355-363.

Sachs, Jacqueline. (1967). Recognition memory for syntactic and semantic aspects of connected discourse. *Perception & Psychophysics*, 1967(2): 437-442.

Schiaffino, Riccardo and Franco Zearo. (2005). Translation Quality Measurement in Practice. 46th ATA Conference, Seattle Technologies.

Stanislaw, Harold and Natasha Todorov. (1999). Calculation of Signal Detection Theory Measures, *Behavior Research Methods, Instruments, & Computers*, 31(1): 137-149.

Takahaski, George. (1969). Perceptions of space and function of certain English prepositions. *Language Learning*, 19: 217-234.

Vilar, David, Jia Xu, Luis Fernando D'Haro, and Hermann Ney. (2006). Error Analysis of Statistical Machine Translation Output. In *Proceedings of the 5th International Conference on Language Resources and Evaluation (LREC'06)*, pp. 697–702, Genoa, Italy

Winer, B., Donald Brown, and Kenneth Michels. (1991). Statistical Principles in Experimental Design. 3rd Edition. New York: McGraw–Hill, Inc. pp. 169-171.

Towards Automatic Lexical Simplification in Spanish: An Empirical Study

Biljana Drndarević and **Horacio Saggion**
Universitat Pompeu Fabra
Department of Information and Communication Technologies
C/ Tanger, 122-140
08018 Barcelona, Spain
{biljana.drndarevic,horacio.saggion}@upf.edu

Abstract

In this paper we present the results of the analysis of a parallel corpus of original and simplified texts in Spanish, gathered for the purpose of developing an automatic simplification system for this language. The system is intended for individuals with cognitive disabilities who experience difficulties reading and interpreting informative texts. We here concentrate on lexical simplification operations applied by human editors on the basis of which we derive a set of rules to be implemented automatically. We have so far addressed the issue of lexical units substitution, with special attention to reporting verbs and adjectives of nationality; insertion of definitions; simplification of numerical expressions; and simplification of named entities.

1 Introduction

In the highly digitalized 21st century sharing information via Internet has become not only commonplace but also essential. Yet, there are still a large number of people who are denied this fundamental human right – access to information. In 2006 the UN conducted an audit with the aim of testing the state of accessibility of the leading websites around the world. The results were rather disappointing, with only three out of 100 tested web pages achieving basic accessibility status. It is therefore clear that one of the priorities for the future is working on enabling inclusion of all the groups that are currently marginalised and denied equal access to information as the rest of the population.

Written information available online is far too often presented in a way that is perceived as incomprehensible to individuals with cognitive disabilities. It is therefore necessary to simplify the complex textual content in order to make it more accessible. However, manual simplification is too time-consuming and little cost-effective so as to yield sufficient amount of simplified reading material in a satisfactory time frame. Hence, the need and interest arise to develop automatic or semi-automatic simplification tools that would (partially) substitute humans in carrying out this laborious task.

Our project is one such aspiration. Our goal is to offer an automated text simplification tool for Spanish, targeted at readers with cognitive disabilities. We delimit our research to simplification of informative texts and news articles. So far we have focused primarily on syntactic simplification, with an already implemented module currently in the test stage (Bott and Saggion, 2012b). The present work, however, deals with lexical simplification and is centred around a corpus analysis, a preparatory stage for the development of a separate lexical module in the future.

Earlier work already establishes the importance of lexical changes for text simplification (Carroll et al., 1998; Caseli et al., 2009; De Belder et al., 2010). Upon examining a parallel corpus consisting of original and manually simplified newspaper articles in Spanish, we have found that by far the most common type of changes applied by human editors are precisely lexical changes, accounting for 17.48% of all annotated operations (Bott and Saggion, 2012a). Words perceived as more complicated are replaced by their simpler synonyms. A recurring example is that of reporting verbs. Corpus analysis shows a clear tendency towards replacing all reporting verbs such as *advertir* (*warn*), *afirmar* (*declare*), *explicar* (*explain*), etc. with the ubiquitous *decir* (*say*). Sentences 1 (original) and 2 (simplified) illustrate the said phenomenon (translated into English):

1. *It is important that we continue working on the means that promote the access of the disabled to cultural content, she* ***explained****.*

2. *The Minister of Culture* ***said*** *that she is working towards granting the disabled access to cultural content.*

We therefore document all cases of lexical change observed in the corpus and try to extract rules for their automatic implementation. The remainder of this paper is organized as follows: Section 2 addresses the related work in the field; in Section 3 we describe the experimental setting and the process of obtaining the parallel corpus used in the study, while Section 4 provides a more detailed insight into the kind of lexical simplifications observed. We conclude in Section 5 and outline our future work.

2 Related Work

Text simplification has so far been approached with two different aims. One is to offer simplified versions of original text to human readers, such as foreign language learners (Petersen and Ostendorf, 2007; Medero and Ostendorf, 2011); aphasic people (Devlin and Unthank, 2006); low literacy individuals (Specia, 2010) and others. On the other hand, simplified text is seen as input for further natural language processing to enhance its proficiency, e.g. in machine translation or information retrieval tools (Klebanov et al., 2004). The earliest simplification systems employed a rule-based approach and focused on syntactic structure of the text (Chandrasekar et al., 1996). The PSET project (Carroll et al., 1998) dealt with simplification of news articles in English for aphasic readers. Together with syntactic analysis and transformations similar to those of Chandrasekar et al. (1996), they employed lexical simplification based on looking up synonyms in WordNet and extracting Kucera-Francis frequency from the Oxford Psycholinguistic Database (Quinlan, 1992). Therefore, the most frequent of a set of synonyms for every content word of the input text was chosen to appear in its simplified version.

The above approach to lexical simplification has been repeated in a number of works (Lal and Ruger, 2002; Burstein et al., 2007). Bautista et al. (2009) also rely on a dictionary of synonyms, but their criterion for choosing the most appropriate one is word-length rather than frequency. Caseli et al. (2009) analyse lexical operations on a parallel corpus of original and manually simplified texts in Portuguese, using lists of simple words and discourse markers as resources. Bautista et al. (2011) focused on numerical expressions as one particular problem of lexical simplification and suggested the use of hedges as a means of dealing with complex numerical content.

Given the fact that many words tend to be polysemic, attempts have been made to address this issue so as to provide more accurate, context-aware lexical substitution. De Belder et al. (2010) were the first to employ word sense disambiguation techniques in order to capture contextual information, while Biran et al. (2011) apply an unsupervised method for learning pairs of complex and simple synonyms based on an unaligned corpus of texts from the original Wikipedia and Simple English Wikipedia.

3 Experimental Setting

We have gathered a corpus consisting of 200 informative texts in Spanish, obtained from the news agency Servimedia. The articles have been classified into four categories: national news, international news, society and culture. We then obtained simplified versions of the said texts, courtesy of the DILES (Discurso y Lengua Española) group of the Autonomous University of Madrid. Simplifications have been applied manually, by trained human editors, following easy-to-read guidelines suggested by Anula (2009), (2008). We are interested to see how these guidelines are applied in practice, as well as how human editors naturally deal with cases not treated by the guidelines in sufficient detail.

The corpus has been automatically annotated using part-of-speech tagging, named entity recognition and parsing (Padró et al., 2010). Furthermore, a text aligning algorithm based on Hidden Markov Models (Bott and Saggion, 2011) has been applied to obtain sentence-level alignments. The automatic alignments have then been manually corrected through a graphical editing tool within the GATE framework (Cunningham et al., 2002). A total of 570 sentences have been aligned (246 in original and 324 in simple texts), with the following correlations between them: *one to one*, *one to many* or *many to one*, as well as cases where there is no correlation (cases of content reduction through summarisation or information expansion through the introduction of definitions). The alignments facilitate the observation of the corpus, particularly cases where entire sentences have been eliminated or inserted.

A parallel corpus thus aligned enables us to engage in data analysis as well as possibly carry out machine learning experiments to treat specific problems we have so far detected. We have documented all simplification operations used by human editors and placed them in eight major categories applied at various linguistic levels (individual words, phrases or sentences). The operations are *change, delete, insert, split, proximization, re-order, select* and *join*, listed in the decreasing order of their relative frequency in the corpus. Among these are the changes that are either rather idiosyncratic or involve complex inferential processes proper to humans but not machines. Sentence 1 (original) and paragraph 2 (simplified) are an example (translated into English):

1. *Around 390,000 people have returned to their homes after being forced to evacuate due to floods caused by monsoon rains last summer in Pakistan.*

2. *Last summer it rained a lot in Pakistan.* ***The rain flooded the fields and the houses. That is to say, the water covered the houses and the fields.*** *For this reason a lot of people left their homes in Pakistan. Now these people return to their homes.*

Sentences in bold are examples of information expansion which is difficult to implement automatically. The concept of flood is obviously perceived as complicated. However, instead of offering a definition taken out of a dictionary and applicable to any context (as in the example further below), the writer explains what happened in this particular instance, relying on their common knowledge and inferential thinking. It is obvious that such conclusions cannot be drawn by computers. What *can* be done is insert a definition of a difficult term, as in the following example:

1. *The Red Cross asks for almost one million euros for the 500,000 Vietnamese affected by the floods.*

2. *The Red Cross asks for one million euros for Vietnam.* ***The Red Cross is an organization that helps people and countries around the world.***

After documenting all the operations and analysing their nature and frequency, we have finally decided to focus on the automatic treatment of the following: lexical simplification, deletions, split operations, inversion of direct speech and the insertion of definitions. In the next section, we concentrate on operations applied at the lexical level, with the aim of drawing conclusions about the nature of lexical simplification carried out by trained editors and the possibility of their automatic implementation in the future.

4 Data Analysis

We have so far obtained forty simplifications and our goal is to shortly acquire simplified versions of all 200 texts. A variety of lexical operations have been observed in the corpus, which go far beyond simple substitution of one lexical unit with its simpler equivalent. In order to describe the nature of these changes, we have categorized them as follows:

- substitutions of one lexical unit with its simpler synonym;
- insertion of definitions of difficult terms and concepts;
- simplification of numerical expressions;
- simplification of named entities;
- elimination of nominalisation;
- rewording of idioms and collocations; and
- rewording of metaphorically used expressions.

4.1 Lexical substitution

We have documented 84 cases where one lexical unit has been substituted with its simpler synonym. These words make up our lexical substitution table (LST), gathered for the purpose of data analysis. The table contains the lemma of the *original* (O) word, its *simple* (S) equivalent and additional information about either the original word, the simple word or the nature of the simplification, such as *polysemy*, *hyponym* ⇒ *hypernym*, *metaphor*, etc. Table 1 is an excerpt.

Original	Simple	Commentary
impartir	pronunciar	polysemy
informar	decir	reporting verb
inmigrante	extranjero	hyponym ⇒ hypernym
letras	literatura	polysemy

Table 1: An excerpt from the Lexical Substitution Table

To analyse the relationship between the sets of O-S words, we have concentrated on their frequency of use and length (both in characters and syllables).

4.1.1 Word frequency

For every word in the LST, we consulted its frequency in a dictionary developed for the purposes of our project by the DILES group and based on the Referential Corpus of Contemporary Spanish (Corpus de Referencia del Español Actual, CREA)[1]. We have found that for 54.76% of the words, the frequency of the simple word is higher than the frequency of its original equivalent; in 30.95% of the cases, the frequency is the same; only 3.57% of the simple words have lower frequency than the corresponding original ones; and in 10.71% of the cases it was impossible to analyse the frequency since the original word was a multi-word expression not included in the dictionary, as is the case with complex conjunctions like *sin embargo* (*however*) or *pese a* (*despite*).

As can be appreciated, in a high number of cases O and S words have the same frequency of use according to CREA. In an intent to rationalise this phenomenon, we have counted the number of times each of these words appears in the totality of original and simple texts. In more than half of the O-S pairs the simple word is more common than its original equivalent, not only in the simplified texts, where it is expected to abound, but also in the original ones. This difference in the frequency of use in actual texts and the CREA database could be explained by the specificity of the genre of the texts in our corpus, where certain words are expected to be recurrent, and the genre-neutral language of CREA on the other hand. Out of the remaining 44.5% of the cases, where O words are more abundant than S words, five out of fourteen may have been used for stylistic purposes. One good example is the use of varied reporting verbs, such as *afirmar* (*confirm*) or *anunciar* (*announce*), instead of uniformly using *decir* (*say*). Six in fourteen of the same group are polysemic words possibly used in contexts other than the one where the simplification was recorded. Such is the example of the word *artículo*, substituted with *cosa* where it meant *thing*. However, it also occurs with its second meaning (*article: a piece of writing*) where it cannot be substituted with *cosa*.

What can be concluded so far is that frequency is a relatively good indicator of the word difficulty, albeit not the only one, as seen by a large number of cases when the pairs of O-S words have the same frequency. For that reason we analyse word length in Section 4.1.2. Polysemy and style are also seen as important factors at the time of deciding on the choice of the synonym to replace a difficult word. Whereas style is a factor we currently do not intend to treat computationally, we cannot but recognize the impact that polysemy has on the quality and accuracy of the output text. Consider the example of another pair of words in our lexical substitution table: *impresión* ⇒ *influencia*, in the following pair of original (1) and simplified (2) sentences:

1. Su propia sede ya da testimonio de la "impresión profunda" que la ciudad andaluza dejó en el pintor.
   Its very setting testifies to the profound influence of the Andalusian town on the painter.

2. En esa casa también se ve la influencia de Granada.
   The influence of Granada is also visible in that house.

In the given context, the two words are perfect syn-

[1] http://corpus.rae.es/creanet.html

onyms. However, in expressions such as *tengo la impresión que* (*I am under the impression that*), the word *impresión* cannot be substituted with *influencia*. We have found that around 35% of all the original words in the LST are polysemic. We therefore believe it is necessary to include a word sense disambiguation approach as part of the lexical simplification component of our system in the future.

4.1.2 Word Length

Table 2 summarizes the findings relative to the word length of the original and simple words in the LST, where *syll.* stands for *syllable* and *char.* for *character*.

Type of relationship	Percentage
S has fewer syll. than O	57.85%
S has more syll. than O	17.85%
S has the same number of syll. as O	25%
S has fewer char. than O	66.66%
S has more char. than O	23.8%
S has the same number of char. as O	9.52%

Table 2: Word length of original and simple words

The average word length in the totality of original texts is 4.81 characters, while the simplified texts contain words of average length of 4.76 characters. We have also found that the original and simplified texts have roughly the same number of short words (up to 5 characters) and medium length words (6-10 characters), while the original texts are more saturated in long words (more than 11 characters) than the simplified ones (5.91% in original and 3.64% in simplified texts). Going back to the words from the LST which had the same frequency according to CREA, we found that around 80% of these were pairs where the simple word had fewer syllables than the original one. This leads us to the conclusion that there is a strong preference for shorter words and that word length is to be combined with frequency when deciding among a set of possible synonyms to replace a difficult word.

4.2 Transformation rules

Upon close observation of our data, we have derived a set of preliminary simplification rules that apply to lexical units substitution. These rules concern reporting verbs and adjectives of nationality, and will be addressed in that order.

In the twenty pairs of aligned texts nine different **reporting verbs** are used. All nine of them have been substituted with *decir* (*say*) at least once, amounting to eleven instances of such substitutions. Three verbs from the same set appear in simplified texts without change. On the whole, we perceive a strong tendency towards using a simple verb like *say* when reporting direct speech. Our intention is to build a lexicon of reporting verbs in Spanish and complement it with grammatical rules so as to enable accurate lexical substitution of these items of vocabulary. Simple substitution of one lexical unit with another is not always possible due to syntactic constraints, as illustrated in the following example:

1. El juez advirtió al duque que podría provocar la citación de la Infanta.
   The judge warned the Duke that he might cause the Princess to be subpoenaed.

2. Murió científico que advirtió sobre deterioro de la capa de ozono.
   The scientist who warned about the deterioration of the ozone layer died.

In the first case the verb *advertir* is used as part of the structure [advertir a X que], in English [warn somebody that]. The verb *decir* easily fits this structure without disturbing the grammaticality of the sentence. In the second instance, however, the reporting verb is used with the preposition and an indirect object, a structure where the insertion of *decir* would be fatal for the grammaticality of the output. We believe that the implementation of this rule would be a worthwhile effort, given that informative texts often abound in direct speech that could be relatively easily simplified so as to enhance readability.

As for **adjectives of nationality**, we have noticed a strong preference for the use of periphrastic structure instead of denominal adjective denoting nationality. Thus, a simple adjective is replaced with the construction [de < COUNTRY >], e.g. *el gobierno pakistaní* (*the Pakistani government*) is replaced by *el gobierno de Pakistán* (*the government of Pakistan*). The same rule is applied to instances of nominalised nationality adjectives. In these cases the structure [ArtDef + Adj][2] be-

[2]ArtDef: definite article, Adj: adjective

comes [ArtDef + persona + de + < COUNTRY >], e.g: *los pakistaníes* ⇒ *las personas de Pakistán* (*the Pakistani* ⇒ *the people from Pakistan*). In only five instances the adjective was preferred. Twice it was *español* (*Spanish*), which were the only two instances of the expression of this nationality. This leads us to the conclusion that *español* is sufficiently widespread and therefore simple enough and would not need to be substituted with its periphrastic equivalent. *Norteamericano* (*North American*) was used twice, therefore being slightly more acceptable than *estadounidense* (*of/from the United States*), which is always replaced by *de Estados Unidos*. The remaining is the one instance of *egipcio* (*Egyptian*), otherwise replaced by *de Egipto*.

Based on the observations, our hypothesis is that more common nationality adjectives, such as *Spanish*, and possibly also *English* or *French* need not be modified. *Norteamericano* or *estadounidense* however common are possibly perceived as complicated due to their length. In order to derive a definite rule, we would need to carry out a more detailed analysis on a richer corpus to determine how frequency of use and length of these adjectives correlate.

4.3 Insertion of definitions

Definitions of difficult terms are found in 57.5% of all texts we have analysed. Around 70% of these are definitions of named entities, such as *El Greco*, *Amnesty International*, *Guantanamo* and others. In addition to these, difficult lexical units, and even expressions, are explained by means of a definition. Thus, *a (prison) cell* is defined as *a room in a prison*, and *the prisoner of conscience* as *a person put in prison for his ideas*. In order to deal with named entity definitions, we intend to investigate the methods for the look-up of such definitions in the future. To solve the problem of defining difficult individual lexical units, one solution is to target those words with the lowest frequency rate and in the absence of an adequate simpler synonym insert a definition from a monolingual dictionary, given the availability of such resources (the definition itself might need to be simplified).

4.4 Numerical expressions

Our analysis shows that the treatment of numerical expressions should have a significant place in our simplification system, given their abundance in the kind of texts our system is mainly intended for, and a wide variety of simplification solutions observed by examining the parallel corpus. Even though by far the most common operation is elimination (in the process of summarization), there are a number of other recurrent operations. The most common of these are explained below for the purpose of illustration, given that the totality of the rules is beyond the scope of this paper. We separately address numerical expressions forming part of a date and other instances of using numbers and numerals.

The following are the rules concerning numerical expressions in dates:

1. en < YEAR > ⇒ en el año < YEAR >
   en 2010 ⇒ en el año 2010

2. Years in parenthesis are eliminated (this operation has been applied in 100% of the cases during manual simplification):
   El Greco (1541–1614) ⇒ El Greco

3. In expressions containing the name and/or the day of the month, irrespective of whether it is followed by a year, the information relative to the month (i.e. name or name and day) is eliminated (applied in around 85% of the cases):
   en septiembre 2010 ⇒ en el año 2010
   el 3 de mayo ⇒ ∅

As for other numerical expressions, the most common rules and most uniformly applied are the following:

1. Replacing a word with a figure:
   cinco días ⇒ 5 días

2. Rounding of big numbers:
   más de 540.000 personas ⇒ medio millón de personas

3. Rounding by elimination of decimal points:
   Cerca de 1,9 millones de casas ⇒ 2 millones de casas

4. Simplification of noun phrases containing two numerals in plural and the preposition *of* by eliminating the first numeral:
   cientos de miles de personas ⇒ miles de personas

5. Substitution of words denoting a certain number of years (such as *decade* or *centenary*) by the corresponding number:
   IV centenario de su nacimiento ⇒ *400 años de su nacimiento*

6. The thousands and millions in big numbers are expressed by means of a word, rather than a figure:
   17.000 *casas* ⇒ 17 *mil casas*

We are currently working on implementing a numerical expression simplification module based on rounding and rewording rules derived from our corpus and previous study in the field (Bautista et al., 2011).

4.5 Named Entities

As with numerical expressions, the majority of named entities are eliminated as a result of summarization. Only those names that are relative to the theme of the text in question and which tend to appear throughout the article are kept. In the case of these examples, we have observed the following operations: abbreviation; disabbreviation; using full name instead of the surname alone, customary in newspaper articles; expanding the noun phrase [ArtDef + NCom][3] with the name of the referent; replacing the noun phrase [ArtDef + NCom] with the name of the referent; inversion of the constituents in the structures where a professional title is followed by the name of its holder in apposition; and a handful of other, less frequent changes. Table 3 summarizes the most common operations and illustrates them with examples from the corpus. As can be observed, some NE are written as acronyms while others are disabbreviated. It would be interesting to analyse in the future whether the length and the relative frequency of the words that make up these expressions are a factor, or these are simply examples of arbitrary choices made by human editors lacking more specific guidelines.

While to decide how to deal with names of organisations that may possibly be abbreviated we would need a larger corpus more saturated in these examples, there are a number of rules ready to be implemented. Such is the case of personal names, where almost 90% of the names appearing in simplified texts contain both name and surname as opposed to first name alone. The same is true of the order of name and title, where in 100% of such examples the name is preferred in the initial position. As for expanding the named entity with a common noun (*the painter Pablo Picasso*), we have recorded this operation in only 15% of the personal names used in S texts. We do, however, notice a pattern — this kind of operation is applied at the first mention of the name, where the common noun acts as an additional defining element. It is an interesting phenomenon to be further researched.

4.6 Other simplification tendencies

Human editors have opted for a number of other simplification solutions which are either difficult or impossible to implement computationally. The elimination of nominalisations is an example of the former. Whereas common in the journalistic genre, human simplifications show a very strong tendency towards substituting the combination of the support verb and a deverbal noun with the corresponding verb alone, as in the example:

1. La financiación ha sido realizada por la Generalitat Valenciana.
   The funding has been provided by the Valencian Government.

2. La Generalitat Valenciana ha financiado la investigación.
   The Valencian Government has financed the research.

The expression *realizar una financiación* (*provide funding*) from the original sentence (1) has been substituted by the verb *financiar* (*to fund*) in the simplified version (2). Twenty other instances of this kind of operation have been recorded, thus making it an issue to be readdressed in the future.

What is also to be addressed is the treatment of set expressions such as idioms and collocations. Although not excessively abundant in the current version of our corpus, we hypothesise that the simplification of such expressions could considerably enhance the readability of the text and the research of the issue could, therefore, prove beneficial, provided

[3]NCom: common noun

Original	Simple	Operation Type
Comité Español de Representates de Personas con Discapacidad	CERMI	abbreviation
el PSOE	el Partido Socialista Obrero Español	disabbreviation
Gonzales-Sinde	Angeles Gonzales-Sinde	full name
el artista	el artista Pablo Picasso	NCom+NE
la ciudad andaluza	Granada	NCom ⇒ NE
La ministra de Defensa, Carme Chacón	Carme Chacón, ministra de Defensa	NCom,NE ⇒ NE,NCom

Table 3: Named Entities Substitution Examples

the availability of the necessary resources for Spanish.

On the other hand, an example of common human simplification tactics which is out of reach for a computational system is rewording of metaphorically used expressions. Thus, *un gigante de la escena* (*a giant on stage*) is changed into *un actor extraordinario* (*an extraordinary actor*). Such examples point out to the limitations automatic simplification systems are bound to possess.

5 Conclusions and future work

In the present paper we have concentrated on the analysis of lexical changes observed in a parallel corpus of original and simplified texts in Spanish. We have categorized all the operations into substitution of lexical units; insertion of definitions of difficult terms and concepts; simplification of numerical expressions; simplification of named entities; and different cases of rewording. Analysis suggests that frequency in combination with word length is the necessary combination of factors to consider when deciding on the choice among a set of synonyms to replace a difficult input word. On the other hand, a high number of polysemic input words underline the importance of including word sense disambiguation as part of the lexical substitution module.

Based on the available data, we have so far derived a set of rules concerning reporting verbs, adjectives of nationality, numerical expressions and named entities, all of which are to be further developed and implemented in the future. Numerical expressions in particular are given an important place in our system and more in-depth analysis is being carried out. We are working on rounding of big numbers and the use of modifiers in the simplification of these expressions. A number of issues are still to be tackled, such as elimination of nominalisation and simplification of multi-word expressions. The ultimate goal is to implement the lexical module as part of a larger architecture of the system for automatic text simplification for Spanish.

Acknowledgements

The present study is part of a Spanish research project entitled Simplext: An automatic system for text simplification (`http://www.simplext.es`). Simplext is led by Technosite and partially funded by the Ministry of Industry, Tourism and Trade of the Government of Spain, through the National Plan for Scientific Research, Development and Technological Innovation (I+D+i), within the strategic Action of Telecommunications and Information Society (Avanza Competitiveness, with the file number TSI-020302-2010-84). We are grateful to the fellowship RYC-2009-04291 from Programa Ramón y Cajal 2009, Ministerio de Economía y Competitividad, Secretaría de Estado de Investigación, Desarrollo e Innovación, Spain.

References

A. Anula. 2008. Lecturas adaptadas a la enseñanza del español como l2: variables lingüísticas para la determinación del nivel de legibilidad. In *La evaluación en el aprendizaje y la enseñanza del español como LE/L2*.

A. Anula. 2009. Tipos de textos, complejidad lingüística y facilicitación lectora. In *Actas del Sexto Congreso de Hispanistas de Asia*, pages 45–61.

S. Bautista, P. Gervás, and R.I. Madrid. 2009. Feasibility analysis for semiautomatic conversion of text to improve readability. In *The Second International Conference on Information and Communication Technologies and Accessibility*.

S. Bautista, R. Hervás, P. Gervás, R. Power, and S. Williams. 2011. How to make numerical information accessible: Experimental identification of simplification strategies. In *Conference on Human-Computer Interaction*, Lisbon, Portugal.

O. Biran, S. Brody, and N. Elhadad. 2011. Putting it simply: a context-aware approach to lexical simplification. In *Proceedings of the 49th Annual Meeting of the Association for Computational Linguistics: Human Language Technologies*, pages 496–501, Portland, Oregon, USA. Association for Computational Linguistics.

S. Bott and H. Saggion. 2011. An unsupervised alignment algorithm for text simplification corpus construction. In *ACL Workshop on Monolingual Text-to-Text Generation*, Portland, USA, June 2011. ACL, ACL.

Stefan Bott and H. Saggion. 2012a. Text simplification tools for spanish. In *Proceedings of Language Resources and Evaluation Conference, 2012*.

Stefan Bott and Horacio Saggion. 2012b. A hybrid system for spanish text simplification. In *Third Workshop on Speech and Language Processing for Assistive Technologies (SLPAT)*, Montreal, Canada.

J. Burstein, J. Shore, J. Sabatini, Yong-Won Lee, and M. Ventura. 2007. The automated text adaptation tool. In *HLT-NAACL (Demonstrations)*, pages 3–4.

J. Carroll, G. Minnen, Y. Canning, S. Devlin, and J. Tait. 1998. Practical simplification of english newspaper text to assist aphasic readers. In *Proc. of AAAI-98 Workshop on Integrating Artificial Intelligence and Assistive Technology*, pages 7–10.

H. M. Caseli, T. F. Pereira, L. Specia, Thiago A. S. Pardo, C. Gasperin, and S. M. Aluísio. 2009. Building a brazilian portuguese parallel corpus of original and simplified texts. In *10th Conference on Intelligent Text PRocessing and Computational Linguistics (CICLing 2009)*.

R. Chandrasekar, D. Doran, and B. Srinivas. 1996. Motivations and methods for text simplification. In *COLING*, pages 1041–1044.

H. Cunningham, D. Maynard, K. Bontcheva, and V. Tablan. 2002. GATE: A framework and graphical development environment for robust NLP tools and applications. In *Proceedings of the 40th Anniversary Meeting of the Association for Computational Linguistics*.

J. De Belder, K. Deschacht, and Marie-Francine Moens. 2010. Lexical simplification. In *Proceedings of Itec2010 : 1st International Conference on Interdisciplinary Research on Technology, Education and Communication*.

S. Devlin and G. Unthank. 2006. Helping aphasic people process online information. In *Proceedings of the 8th international ACM SIGACCESS conference on Computers and accessibility*, Assets '06, pages 225–226, New York, NY, USA.

B. B. Klebanov, K. Knight, and D. Marcu. 2004. Text simplification for information-seeking applications. In *On the Move to Meaningful Internet Systems, Lecture Notes in Computer Science*, pages 735–747.

P. Lal and S. Ruger. 2002. Extract-based summarization with simplification. In *Proceedings of the ACL 2002 Automatic Summarization / DUC 2002 Workshop*.

J. Medero and M. Ostendorf. 2011. Identifying targets for syntactic simplification.

Ll. Padró, M. Collado, S. Reese, M. Lloberes, and I. Castellón. 2010. Freeling 2.1: Five years of open-source language processing tools. In *Proceedings of the Seventh International Conference on Language Resources and Evaluation (LREC'10)*, Valletta, Malta.

S. E. Petersen and M. Ostendorf. 2007. Text simplification for language learners: a corpus analysis. In *Proc. of Workshop on Speech and Language Technology for Education*.

P. Quinlan. 1992. *The Oxford Psycholinguistic Database*. Oxford University Press.

Lucia Specia. 2010. Translating from complex to simplified sentences. In *Proceedings of the 9th international conference on Computational Processing of the Portuguese Language*, pages 30–39, Berlin, Heidelberg.

Offline Sentence Processing Measures for testing Readability with Users

Advaith Siddharthan
Department of Computing Science
University of Aberdeen
advaith@abdn.ac.uk

Napoleon Katsos
Department of Theoretical and Applied Linguistics
University of Cambridge
nk248@cam.ac.uk

Abstract

While there has been much work on computational models to predict readability based on the lexical, syntactic and discourse properties of a text, there are also interesting open questions about how computer generated text should be evaluated with target populations. In this paper, we compare two offline methods for evaluating sentence quality, magnitude estimation of acceptability judgements and sentence recall. These methods differ in the extent to which they can differentiate between surface level fluency and deeper comprehension issues. We find, most importantly, that the two correlate. Magnitude estimation can be run on the web without supervision, and the results can be analysed automatically. The sentence recall methodology is more resource intensive, but allows us to tease apart the fluency and comprehension issues that arise.

1 Introduction

In Natural Language Generation, recent approaches to evaluation tend to consider either "naturalness" or "usefulness". Following evaluation methodologies commonly used for machine translation and summarisation, there have been attempts to measure naturalness in NLG by comparison to human generated gold standards. This has particularly been the case in evaluating referring expressions, where the generated expression can be treated as a set of attributes and compared with human generated expressions (Gatt et al., 2009; Viethen and Dale, 2006), but there have also been attempts at evaluating sentences this way. For instance, Langkilde-Geary (2002) generate sentences from a parsed analysis of an existing sentence, and evaluate by comparison to the original. However, this approach has been criticised at many levels (see for example, Gatt et al. (2009) or Sripada et al. (2003)); for instance, because there are many good ways to realise a sentence, because typical NLG tasks do not come with reference sentences, and because fluency judgements in the monolingual case are more subtle than for machine translation.

Readability metrics, by comparison, do not rely on reference texts, and try to model the linguistic quality of a text based on features derived from the text. This body of work ranges from the Flesch Metric (Flesch, 1951), which is based on average word and sentence length, to more systematic evaluations of various lexical, syntactic and discourse characteristics of a text (cf. Pitler et al. (2010), who assess readability of textual summaries). Some researchers have also suggested measuring edit distance by using a human to revise a system generated text and quantifying the revisions made (Sripada et al., 2003). This does away with the need for reference texts and is quite suited to expert domains such as medicine or weather forecasting, where a domain expert can easily correct system output. Analysis of these corrections can provide feedback on problematic content and style. We have previously evaluated text reformulation applications by asking readers which version they prefer (Siddharthan et al., 2011), or through the use of Likert scales (Likert, 1932) for measuring meaning preservation and grammaticality (Siddharthan, 2006). However, none of these approaches tell us very much about the comprehensibility of a text for an end reader.

To address this, there has been recent interest in task based evaluations. Task based evaluations directly evaluate generated utterances for their utility to the hearer. However, while for some generation areas like reference (Gatt et al., 2009), the real world evaluation task is obvious, it is less so for other generation tasks such as surface realisation or text-to-text regeneration or paraphrase. We are thus keen to investigate psycholinguistic methods for investigating sentence processing as an alternative to task based evaluations.

In the psycholinguistics literature, various offline and online techniques have been used to investigate sentence processing by readers. Online techniques (eye-tracking (Duchowski, 2007), neurophysiological (Friederici, 1995), etc.) offer many advantages in studying how readers process a sentence. But as these are difficult to set up and also resource intensive, we would prefer to evaluate NLG using offline techniques. Some offline techniques, such as Cloze tests (Taylor, 1953) or question answering, require careful preparation of material (choice of texts and questions, and for Cloze, the words to leave out). Other methods, such as magnitude estimation and sentence recall (cf. Sec 3 for details), are more straightforward to implement. In this paper, we investigate magnitude estimation of acceptability judgements and delayed sentence recall in the context of an experiment investigating generation choices when realising causal relations. Our goal is to study how useful these methods are for evaluating surface level fluency and deeper comprehensibility. We are interested in whether they can distinguish between similar sentences, and whether they can be used to test hypotheses regarding the effect of common generation decisions such as information order and choice of discourse marker. We briefly discuss the data in Section 2, before describing our experiments (Sections 3.1 and 3.2). We finish with a discussion of their suitability for more general evaluation of NLG with target readers.

2 Data

We use a dataset created to explore generation choices in the context of expressing causal relations; specifically, the choice of periphrastic causative (Wolff et al., 2005) and information order. The dataset considers four periphrastic causatives (henceforth referred to as discourse markers): "*because*", "*because of*", the verb "*cause*" and the noun "*cause*" with different lexico-syntactic properties. We present an example from this dataset below (cf. Siddharthan and Katsos (2010) for details):

(1) a. Fructose-induced hypertension **is caused by** increased salt absorption by the intestine and kidney. **[b_caused-by_a]**

b. Increased salt absorption by the intestine and kidney **causes** fructose-induced hypertension. **[a_caused_b]**

c. Fructose-induced hypertension occurs **because of** increased salt absorption by the intestine and kidney. **[b_because-of_a]**

d. **Because of** increased salt absorption by the intestine and kidney, fructose-induced hypertension occurs. **[because-of_ab]**

e. Fructose-induced hypertension occurs **because** there is increased salt absorption by the intestine and kidney. **[b_because_a]**

f. **Because** there is increased salt absorption by the intestine and kidney, fructose-induced hypertension occurs. **[because_ab]**

g. Increased salt absorption by the intestine and kidney is the **cause of** fructose-induced hypertension. **[a_cause-of_b]**

h. The **cause of** fructose-induced hypertension is increased salt absorption by the intestine and kidney. **[cause-of_ba]**

In this notation, "a" represents the cause,"b" represents the effect and the remaining string indicates the discourse marker; their ordering reflects the information order in the sentence, for example, "a_cause-of_b" indicates a cause-effect information order using "cause of" as the discourse marker. The dataset consists of 144 sentences extracted from corpora (18 sentences in each condition (discourse marker + information order), reformulated manually to generated the other seven conditions, resulting in 1152 sentences in total.

Clearly, different formulations have different levels of fluency. In this paper we explore what two offline sentence processing measures can tell us about their acceptability and ease of comprehension.

3 Method

3.1 Magnitude estimation of acceptability

Human judgements for acceptability for each of the 1152 sentences in the dataset were obtained using the WebExp package (Keller et al., 2009). Note that the reformulations are, strictly speaking, grammatical according to the authors' judgement. We are testing violations of acceptability, rather than grammaticality per se. This mirrors the case of NLG, where a grammar is often used for surface realisation, ensuring grammaticality.

Acceptability is a measure which reflects both ease of comprehension and surface well-formedness. We later compare this experiment with a more qualitative comprehension experiment based on sentence recall (cf. Section 3.2). Rather than giving participants a fixed scale, we used the magnitude estimation paradigm, which is more suitable to capture robust or subtle differences between the relative strength of acceptability or grammaticality violations (see, for example, Bard et al. (1996); Cowart (1997); Keller (2000)). One advantage of magnitude estimation is that the researcher does not make any assumptions about the number of linguistic distinctions allowed. Each participant makes as many distinctions as they feel comfortable. Participants were given the following instructions (omitting those that relate to the web interface):

1. Judge acceptability of construction, not of meaning;
2. There is no limit to the set of numbers you can use, but they must all be positive - the lowest score you can assign is 0. In other words, make as many distinctions as you feel comfortable;
3. Always score the new sentence relative to the score you gave the modulus sentence, which you will see on the top of the screen;
4. Acceptability is a continuum, do not just make yes/no judgements on grammaticality;
5. Try not to use a fixed scale, such as 1–5, which you might have used for other linguistic tasks previously.

Design: The propositional content of 144 sentences was presented in eight conditions. Eight participant groups (A–H) consisting of 6 people each were presented with exactly one of the eight formulations of each of 144 different sentences, as per a Latin square design. This experimental design allows all statistical comparisons between the eight types of causal formulations and the three genres to be within-participant. The participants were University of Cambridge students (all native English speakers). Participants were asked to score how acceptable a modulus sentence was, using any positive number. They were then asked to score other sentences relative to this modulus, so that higher scores were assigned to more acceptable sentences. Scores were normalised to allow comparison across participants, following standard practice in the literature, by using the z-score: For each participant, each sentence score was normalised so that the mean score is 0 and the standard deviation is 1 ($z_{ih} = \frac{x_{ih}-\mu_h}{\sigma_h}$), where z_{ih} is participant h's z-score for the sentence i when participant h gave a magnitude estimation score of x_{ih} to that sentence. μ_h is the mean and σ_h the standard deviation of the set of magnitude estimation scores for user h.

3.2 Sentence Recall

Acceptability ratings are regarded as a useful measure because they combine surface judgements of grammaticality with deeper judgements about how easy a sentence is to understand. However, one might want to know whether an inappropriate formulation can cause a breakdown in comprehension of the content of a sentence, which would go beyond the (perhaps) non-detrimental effect of a form that is dispreferred at the surface level. To try and learn more about this, we conducted a second behavioural experiment using a sentence recall methodology. As these experiments are harder to conduct and have to be supervised in a lab (to ensure that participants have similar conditions of attention and motivation, and to prevent "cheating" using cut-and-paste or note taking techniques), we selected a subset of 32 pairs of items from the previous experiment. Each pair consisted of two formulations of the same sentence. The pairs were selected in a manner that exhibited a variation in the within-pair difference of acceptability. In other words, we wanted to explore whether two formulations of a sentences with similar acceptability ratings were recalled equally well and whether two formulations of a sentence with different acceptability ratings were recalled differently.

Design: 32 students at the University of Cambridge were recruited (these are different participants from those in the acceptability experiment in Section 3.1, but were also all native speakers). We created four groups A–D, each with eight participants. Each Group saw 16 sentences in exactly one of the two formulation types, such that groups A–B formed one Latin square and C–D formed another Latin square. These 16 sentences were interleaved with 9 filler sentences that did not express causality. For each item, a participant was first shown a sentence on the screen at the rate of 0.5 seconds per word. Then, the sentence was removed from the screen, and the participant was asked to do two arithmetic tasks (addition and subtraction of numbers between 10 and 99). The purpose of these tasks was to add a load between target sentence and recall so that the recall of the target sentence could not rely on internal rehearsal of the sentence. Instead, research suggests that in such conditions recall is heavily dependent on whether the content and form was actually comprehended (Lombardi and Potter, 1992; Potter and Lombardi, 1990). Participants then typed what they recalled of the sentence into a box on the screen.

We manually coded the recalled sentences for six error types (1–6) or perfect recall (0) as shown in Table 1. Further, we scored the sentences based on our judgements of how bad each error-type was. The table also shows the weight for each error type. For any recalled sentences, only one of (0,1,5,6) is coded, i.e., these codes are mutually exclusive, but if none of the positive scores (0,1,5,6) have been coded, any combination of error types (2,3,4) can be coded for the same sentence.

4 Results

4.1 Correlation between the two methods

The correlation between the differences in acceptability (using average z-scores for each formulation from the magnitude estimation experiment) and recall scores (scored as described above) for the 32 pairs of sentences was found to be significant (Spearman's rho=.43; p=.01). A manual inspection of the data showed up one major issue regarding the methodologies: our participants appear to penalise perceived ungrammaticalities in short sentences quite harshly when rating acceptability, but they have no trouble recalling such sentences accurately. For example, sentence a. in Example 2 below had an average acceptability score of 1.41, while sentence b. only scored .13, but both sentences were recalled perfectly by all participants in the recall study:

(2) a. It is hard to imagine that it was the cause of much sadness.

b. It is hard to imagine that because of it there was much sadness.

Indeed the sentence recall test failed to discriminate at all for sentences under 14 words in length. When we removed pairs with sentences under 14 words (there were eight such pairs), the correlation between the differences in magest and recall scores for the 24 remaining pairs of sentences was even stronger (Spearman's rho=.64; p<.001).

Summary: The two methodologies give very different results for short sentences. This is because comprehension is rarely an issue for short sentences, while surface level disfluencies are more jarring to participants in such short sentences. For longer sentences, the two methods correlate strongly; for such sentences, magnitude estimations of acceptability better reflect ease of comprehension. In retrospect, this suggests that the design of an appropriate load (we used two arithmetic sums) is an important consideration that can affect the usefulness of recall measures. One could argue that acceptability is a more useful metric for evaluating NLG as it combines surface level fluency judgements with ease of comprehension issues. In Siddharthan and Katsos (2010), we described how this data could be used to train an NLG component to select the most acceptable formulation of a sentence expressing a causal relation. We now enumerate other characteristics of magnitude estimation of acceptability that make them useful for evaluating sentences. Then, in Section 4.3, we discuss what further information can be gleaned from sentence recall studies.

4.2 Results of magnitude estimation study

Distinguishing between sentences: We found that magnitude estimation judgements are very good at distinguishing sentences expressing the same content. Consider Table 2, which shows the average acceptability for the n-best formulation of each of the

Weight	Error Code	Error Description
+0.5	0	Recalled accurately (clauses A and B can be valid paraphrases, but the discourse connective (TYPE) is the same)
+0.4	1	Clauses A and B are recalled accurately but the relation is reformulated using a different *but valid* discourse marker
-0.25	2	The discourse marker has been changed in a manner that modifies the original causal relation
-0.5	3	Clause B (effect) recall error (clause is garbled)
-0.5	4	Clause A (cause) recall error (clause is garbled)
+0.25	5	Causal relation and A and B are recalled well, but some external modifying clause is not recalled properly
+0.25	6	Causality is quantified (e.g., "major cause") and this modifier is lost or changed in recall (valid paraphrases are not counted here)

Table 1: Weighting function for error types.

144 sentences (n=1–8). We see that the best formulation averages .89, the second best .57 and the worst formulation -.90. Note that it is not always the same formulation types that are deemed acceptable – if we always select the most preferred type (a_caused_b) for each of the 144 sentences, the average acceptability is only .12.

n =	1	2	3	4	5	6	7	8
Av. Z =	.89	.57	.33	.13	-.12	-.33	-.58	-.90

Table 2: Average acceptability for the nth best formulation of each of the 144 sentences.

Testing hypotheses: In addition to distinguishing between different formulations of a sentence, varying generation choices systematically allows us to test any hypotheses we might have about their effect on acceptability. Indeed, hypothesis testing was an important consideration in the design of this experiment. For instance, various studies (Clark and Clark, 1968; Katz and Brent, 1968; Irwin, 1980) suggest that for older school children, college students and adults, comprehension is better for the cause-effect presentation, both when the relation is implicit (no discourse marker) and explicit (with a discourse marker). We can then test specific predictions about which formulations are likely to be more acceptable.

H1 We expect the cause-effect information order to be deemed more acceptable than the corresponding effect-cause information order.

H2 As all four discourse markers are commonly used in language, we do not expect any particular marker to be globally preferred to the others.

We ran a 4 (discourse marker) x 2 (information order) repeated measures ANOVA. We found a main effect of information order (F1(1, 49) = 5.19, p = .017) and discourse marker (F1(3, 147) = 3.48, p = .027). Further, we found a strong interaction between information order and formulation type, F1(3, 147) = 19.17, p<.001. We now discuss what these results mean.

Understanding generation decisions: The main effect of discourse marker was not predicted (Hypothesis H2). We could try and explain this empirically. For instance, in the BNC "because" as a conjunction occurs 741 times per million words, while "cause" as a verb occurs 180 times per million words, "because of" 140 per million words and "cause" as a noun 86 per million words. We might expect the more common markers to be judged more acceptable. However, there was no significant correlation between participants' preference for discourse marker and the BNC corpus frequencies of the markers (Spearman's rho=0.4, p>0.75). This suggests that corpus frequencies need not be a reliable indicator of reader preferences, at least for discourse connectives. The mean z-scores for the four discourse markers are presented in Table 3

To explore the interaction between discourse marker and information order, a post-ANOVA Tukey HSD analysis was performed. The significant

Discourse Marker	Average Z-score
Cause (verb)	0.036
Because of	0.028
Because	-0.011
Cause (noun)	-0.028

Table 3: Av. z-scores for the four discourse markers

effects are listed in Table 4. There is a significant preference for using "because" and "because of" in the effect-cause order (infix) over the cause-effect order (prefix) and for using "cause" as a verb in the cause-effect order (active voice) over the effect-cause order (passive voice). Thus, hypothesis H1 is not valid for "because" and "because of", where the canonical infix order is preferred, and though there are numerical preferences for the cause-effect order for "cause" as a noun we found support for hypothesis H1 to be significant only for "cause" as a verb. Table 4 also tells us that if the formulation is in cause-effect order, there is a preference for "cause" as a verb over "because" and "because of". On the other hand, if the formulation is in the reverse effect-cause order, there is a preference for "because" or "because of" over "cause" as a verb or as a noun.

Summary: This evaluation provides us with some insights into how generation decisions interact, which can be used prescriptively to, for example, select a discourse marker, given a required information order.

4.3 Results of sentence recall study

While magnitude estimation assessments of acceptability can be used to test some hypotheses about the effect of generation decisions, it cannot really tease apart cases where there are surface level disfluencies from those that result in a breakdown in comprehension. To test such hypotheses, we use the sentence recall study.

Testing hypotheses: Previous research (e.g., Engelkamp and Rummer (2002)) suggests that recall for the second clause is worse when clauses are combined through coordination (such as "therefore" or "and") than through subordination such as "because". The explanation is that subordination better unifies the two clauses in immediate memory. We would expect this unification to be even greater when the cause and effect are arguments to a verb. Thus, compared to "because", we would expect recall of the second clause to be higher for "cause" as a verb or a noun, due to the tighter syntactic binding to the discourse marker (object of a verb). Likewise, compared to "cause", we would expect to see more recall errors for the second clause when using "because" as a conjunction. Our hypotheses are listed below:

H3 For "cause" as a verb or a noun, there will be fewer recall errors in "a" and "b" compared to "because" or "because of", because of the tighter syntactic binding.

H4 For "because" as a conjunction, there will be more recall errors in the second clause than in the first clause; i.e., for "b_because_a", clause "a" will have more recall errors than "b" and for "because_ab", clause "a" will have fewer recall errors than "b".

Table 5 shows the average incidence of each error type per sentences in that formulation (cf. Table 1). Note that the totals per row might add up to slightly more than 1 because multiple errors can be coded for the same sentence.

Table 5 shows that "because" and "because of" constructs result in more type 3 and 4 recall errors in clauses "a" and/or "b" compared with "cause" as either a noun or a verb. This difference is significant (z-test; $p<.001$), thus supporting hypothesis H3.

Further, for "because", the recall errors for the first clause are significantly fewer than for the second clause (z-test; $p<.01$), thus supporting hypothesis H4. In contrast, for the cases with "cause" as a verb or noun, both A and B are arguments to a verb (either "cause" or a copula), and the tighter syntactic binding helps unify them in immediate memory, resulting in fewer recall errors that are also distributed more evenly between the first and the second argument to the verb.

We make one further observation: passive voice sentences appear to be reformulated at substantial levels (19%), but in a valid manner (type 1 errors). This suggests that the dispreference for passives in the acceptability study is about surface level form rather than deeper comprehension. This would be a

(a) Ordering Effects

Marker	Preference	p-value
because	**effect-cause (.12) is preferred over cause-effect (-.14)**	p<.001
because of	**effect-cause (.13) is preferred over cause-effect (-.11)**	p<.001
cause (verb)	**cause-effect (.12) is preferred over effect-cause (-.05)**	p=.0145
cause (noun)	cause-effect (.01) is preferred over effect-cause (-.11)	p=.302

(b) Discourse Marker Effects

Order	Preference	p-value
effect-cause	**'because' (.12) is preferred over 'cause (noun)' (-.11)**	p<.001
effect-cause	**'because-of' (.13) is preferred over 'cause (noun)' (-.11)**	p<.001
effect-cause	**'because-of' (.13) is preferred over 'cause (verb)' (-.05)**	p=.001
effect-cause	**'because' (.12) is preferred over 'cause (verb)' (-.05)**	p=.002
effect-cause	'cause (verb)' (-.05) is preferred over 'cause (noun)' (-.11)	p=.839
effect-cause	'because' (.12) is preferred over 'because-of' (.13)	p=.999
cause-effect	**'cause (verb)' (.13) is preferred over 'because' (-.14)**	p<.001
cause-effect	**' cause (verb)' (.13) is preferred over 'because-of' (-.06)**	p=.006
cause-effect	'cause (verb)' (.13) is preferred over 'cause (noun)' (.01)	p=.165
cause-effect	'cause (noun)' (.01) is preferred over 'because' (-.14)	p=.237
cause-effect	'because-of' (-.06) is preferred over 'because' (-.14)	p=.883
cause-effect	'cause (noun)' (.01) is preferred over 'because-of' (-.06)	p=.961

Table 4: Interaction effects between information order and discourse marker (mean z-scores in parentheses; significant effects in bold face).

reasonable conclusion, given that all our participants are university students.

Summary: Overall we conclude that sentence recall studies provide insights into the nature of the comprehension problems encountered, and they corroborate acceptability ratings in general, and particularly so for longer sentences.

5 Conclusions

In this paper, we have tried to separate out surface form aspects of acceptability from breakdowns in comprehension, using two offline psycholinguistic methods.

We believe that sentence recall methodologies can substitute for task based evaluations and highlight breakdowns in comprehension at the sentence level. However, like most task based evaluations, recall experiments are time consuming as they need to be conducted in a supervised setting. Additionally, they require manual annotation of error types, though perhaps this could be automated.

Acceptability ratings on the other hand are easy to acquire. Based on our experiments, we believe that acceptability ratings are reliable indicators of comprehension for longer sentences and, particularly for shorter sentences, combine surface form judgements with ease of comprehension in a manner that is very relevant for evaluating sentence generation or regeneration, including simplification.

Both methods are considerably easier to set up and interpret than online methods such as self paced reading, eye tracking or neurophysiological methods.

Acknowledgements

This work was supported by the Economic and Social Research Council (Grant Number RES-000-22-3272).

References

E.G. Bard, D. Robertson, and A. Sorace. 1996. Magnitude estimation for linguistic acceptability. *Language*, 72(1):32–68.

H.H. Clark and E.V. Clark. 1968. Semantic distinctions and memory for complex sentences. *The Quarterly Journal of Experimental Psychology*, 20(2):129–138.

type	err0	err1	err2	err3	err4	err5	err6
b_because_a	0.62	0.18	0.02	0.10	0.18	0.00	0.05
because_ab	0.80	0.03	0.03	0.20	0.10	0.00	0.00
b_because-of_a	0.78	0.11	0.02	0.06	0.07	0.00	0.06
because-of_ab	0.73	0.00	0.00	0.17	0.17	0.10	0.00
a_cause-of_b	0.89	0.04	0.06	0.00	0.00	0.00	0.07
cause-of_ba	0.75	0.06	0.04	0.06	0.08	0.00	0.06
a_caused_b	0.83	0.05	0.02	0.03	0.03	0.07	0.00
b_caused-by_a	0.77	0.19	0.00	0.00	0.04	0.00	0.02

Table 5: Table of recall errors per type.

W. Cowart. 1997. *Experimental Syntax: applying objective methods to sentence judgement*. Thousand Oaks, CA: Sage Publications.

A.T. Duchowski. 2007. *Eye tracking methodology: Theory and practice*. Springer-Verlag New York Inc.

J. Engelkamp and R. Rummer. 2002. Subordinating conjunctions as devices for unifying sentences in memory. *European Journal of Cognitive Psychology*, 14(3):353–369.

Rudolf Flesch. 1951. *How to test readability*. Harper and Brothers, New York.

A.D. Friederici. 1995. The time course of syntactic activation during language processing: A model based on neuropsychological and neurophysiological data. *Brain and language*, 50(3):259–281.

A. Gatt, A. Belz, and E. Kow. 2009. The tuna-reg challenge 2009: Overview and evaluation results. In *Proceedings of the 12th European workshop on natural language generation*, pages 174–182. Association for Computational Linguistics.

J.W. Irwin. 1980. The effects of explicitness and clause order on the comprehension of reversible causal relationships. *Reading Research Quarterly*, 15(4):477–488.

E.W. Katz and S.B. Brent. 1968. Understanding connectives. *Journal of Verbal Learning & Verbal Behavior*.

F. Keller, S. Gunasekharan, N. Mayo, and M. Corley. 2009. Timing accuracy of web experiments: A case study using the WebExp software package. *Behavior Research Methods*, 41(1):1.

Frank Keller. 2000. *Gradience in Grammar: Experimental and Computational Aspects of Degrees of Grammaticality*. Ph.D. thesis, University of Edinburgh.

I. Langkilde-Geary. 2002. An empirical verification of coverage and correctness for a general-purpose sentence generator. In *Proceedings of the 12th International Natural Language Generation Workshop*, pages 17–24. Citeseer.

R. Likert. 1932. A technique for the measurement of attitudes. *Archives of psychology*.

L. Lombardi and M.C. Potter. 1992. The regeneration of syntax in short term memory* 1. *Journal of Memory and Language*, 31(6):713–733.

E. Pitler, A. Louis, and A. Nenkova. 2010. Automatic evaluation of linguistic quality in multi-document summarization. In *Proceedings of the 48th Annual Meeting of the Association for Computational Linguistics*, pages 544–554. Association for Computational Linguistics.

M.C. Potter and L. Lombardi. 1990. Regeneration in the short-term recall of sentences* 1. *Journal of Memory and Language*, 29(6):633–654.

Advaith Siddharthan and Napoleon Katsos. 2010. Reformulating discourse connectives for non-expert readers. In *Proceedings of the 11th Annual Conference of the North American Chapter of the Association for Computational Linguistics (NAACL-HLT 2010)*, Los Angeles, CA.

A. Siddharthan, A. Nenkova, and K. McKeown. 2011. Information status distinctions and referring expressions: An empirical study of references to people in news summaries. *Computational Linguistics*, 37(4):811–842.

Advaith Siddharthan. 2006. Syntactic simplification and text cohesion. *Research on Language and Computation*, 4(1):77–109.

S. Sripada, E. Reiter, and I. Davy. 2003. SumTime-Mousam: Configurable marine weather forecast generator. *Expert Update*, 6(3):4–10.

W.L. Taylor. 1953. " cloze procedure": a new tool for measuring readability. *Journalism Quarterly; Journalism Quarterly*.

Jette Viethen and Robert Dale. 2006. Algorithms for generating referring expressions: do they do what people do? In *Proceedings of the Fourth International Natural Language Generation Conference*, pages 63–70.

P. Wolff, B. Klettke, T. Ventura, and G. Song. 2005. Expressing causation in English and other languages. *Categorization inside and outside the laboratory: Essays in honor of Douglas L. Medin*, pages 29–48.

Graphical Schemes May Improve Readability but Not Understandability for People with Dyslexia

Luz Rello,[1,2] **Horacio Saggion**[2]
[1] Web Research Group
[2] NLP Research Group
Universitat Pompeu Fabra, Barcelona
luzrello@acm.org
horacio.saggion@upf.edu

Ricardo Baeza-Yates, Eduardo Graells
Web Research Group
Universitat Pompeu Fabra
Yahoo! Research, Barcelona
rbaeza@acm.org
eduardo.graells@upf.edu

Abstract

Generally, people with dyslexia are poor readers but strong visual thinkers. The use of graphical schemes for helping text comprehension is recommended in education manuals. This study explores the relation between text readability and the visual conceptual schemes which aim to make the text more clear for these specific target readers. Our results are based on a user study for Spanish native speakers through a group of twenty three dyslexic users and a control group of similar size. The data collected from our study combines qualitative data from questionnaires and quantitative data from tests carried out using eye tracking. The findings suggest that graphical schemes may help to improve readability for dyslexics but are, unexpectedly, counterproductive for understandability.

1 Introduction

Readability refers to the legibility of a text, that is, the ease with which text can be read. On the other hand, understandability refers to comprehensibility, the ease with which text can be understood. Since readability strongly affects text comprehension (Barzilay et al., 2002), sometimes both terms have been used interchangeably (Inui et al., 2003). However, previous research with dyslexic people have shown that both concepts need to be taken into consideration separately. For instance, while in dyslexic population reading, comprehension has been found to be independent of the spelling errors of the text; lexical quality can be used as an indicator of understandability for the non-dyslexic population (Rello and Baeza-Yates, 2012).

Dyslexia has been defined both as a specific reading disability (Vellutino et al., 2004) and as a learning disability (International Dyslexia Association, 2011). It is neurological in origin and it is characterized by difficulties with accurate and/or fluent word recognition and by poor spelling and decoding abilities. Secondary consequences include problems in reading comprehension and reduced reading experience that can impede growth of vocabulary and background knowledge (International Dyslexia Association, 2011).

On the other hand, the role of visual thinking is crucial in dyslexics and its development may be helpful for a number of tasks such as visual analysis and pattern recognition (West, 2009). Partially related to the importance of visual thinking in dyslexics, the use of graphical schemes has been an extensively recommended pedagogical strategy for dyslexic students (Ramírez Sánchez, 2011; Chalkley et al., 2001) as well as for students with reading disabilities (López Castro, 2010).

The inclusion of semantic maps was found to be beneficial for reading comprehension of general disabled readers in (Sinatra et al., 1984) and the inclusion of graphical schemes to improve comprehension for dyslexic readers has been proposed in (Weaver, 1978). However, to the best of our knowledge, no estimation of the effect of graphical schemes on the readability for dyslexics using eye tracking together with their effect in understandability has been done. Therefore, this paper presents the following three main contributions for Spanish native speakers:

- An estimation of the effect of graphical schemes in the readability of dyslexic readers based on the analysis of an eye tracking user study.
- The relationship between readability and understandability in dyslexic readers using comprehension questionnaires.
- A survey conducted among dyslexics on the helpfulness of including graphical schemes.

The rest of the paper is organized as follows. Section 2 covers related work and Section 3 details the experimental methodology. Section 4 presents our results and in Section 5 conclusions and future challenges are drawn.

2 Related Work

We divide the related work in: (1) strategies used in discourse simplification for dyslexics, and (2) how these strategies were measured in relationship with readability and understandability.

Since dyslexics represent a target population of poor readers, different strategies have been applied for improving readability: the use of different text formats (Rello et al., 2012) and environments (Gregor and Newell, 2000), the use of multi-modal information (Kiraly and Ridge, 2001) and text to speech technologies (Elkind et al., 1993), among others. The closest work to ours is the incorporation of summaries and graphical schemes in texts. Previous work has shown that the readability of dyslexic students could be improved by using text summarization (Nandhini and Balasundaram, 2011) and semantic maps (Sinatra et al., 1984).

Various factors have been applied to measure readability in dyslexics. Classic readability measures are useful to find appropriate reading material for dyslexics (Kotula, 2003) and to measure comprehension. For instance, the Flesch-Kincaid readability degree was applied to access comprehension speeds and accuracy in dyslexic readers (Kurniawan and Conroy, 2006). Other specific readability measures for dyslexic readers have been proposed in other domains such as information retrieval (Sitbon and Bellot, 2008).

In the case of the use of summaries, the evaluation of comprehension was carried out using questionnaires (Nandhini and Balasundaram, 2011). Multiple choice questions were applied to measure the incorporation of semantic maps among disable readers (Sinatra et al., 1984) and eye tracking measures have been used to explore various characteristics related to dyslexic reading (Eden et al., 1994).

Although the creation of graphical schemes is extensively recommended in literature (Weaver, 1978; Ramírez Sánchez, 2011; López Castro, 2010), we found no formal evaluation of their impact in readability and comprehension combining data from eye tracking, questionnaires, and a survey.

3 Experimental Methodology

3.1 Participants

Twenty three native Spanish speakers with a confirmed diagnosis of dyslexia took part in the study, twelve of whom were female and eleven male. All the participants were asked to bring their diagnoses to the experiment. Their ages ranged from 13 to 37, with a mean age of 20.74. There were three participants with attention deficit disorder. All participants were frequent readers; eleven read less than four hours per day, nine read between four and eight hours per day, and three participants read more than eight hours daily. Ten people were studying or already finished university degrees, eleven were attending school or high school and two had no higher education. A control group of 23 participants without dyslexia and similar age average (20.91) also participated in the experiment.

3.2 Design

The experiment was composed of four parts: (1) an initial interview designed to collect demographic information, (2) a reading test, (3) two questionnaires designed to control the comprehension, and (4) a survey to know the impressions of each person regarding the inclusion of graphical schemes.

Along the reading test we collected the quantitative data to measure readability, with the comprehension questionnaires we measure understandability, while with the survey we gather information about the participant views.

We used two different variants (A and B) of the

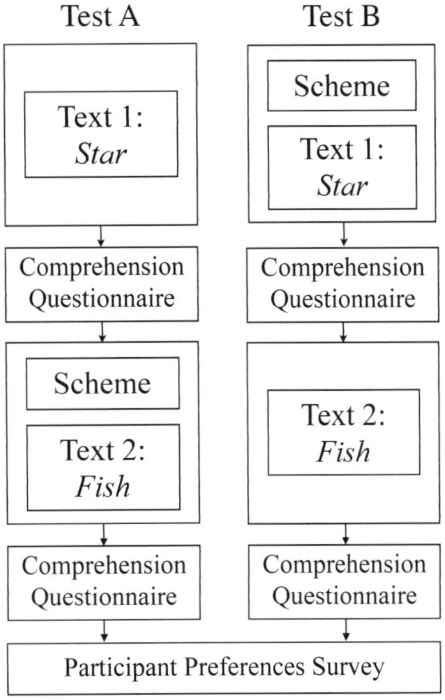

Figure 1: Variants of the experiment.

test (see Figure 1). Each test was composed of two texts: one text that included a graphical scheme in the top and another text without the graphical scheme. We extracted the most similar texts we could find from the Spanish Simplex corpus (Bott and Saggion, 2012). The chosen texts share the following characteristics:

(a) They both have the same genre: science news.

(b) They are about similar topics: Text 1 (called *Star*) is about the discovery of a supernova and text 2 (*Fish*) is about the discovery of a new species of fish.

(c) They contain the same number of sentences: 4 sentences in addition to the title.

(d) They have the same number of words (136).

(e) They have a similar average word length: 5.06 letters per word in *Star* and 5.12 letters per word in *Fish*.

(f) They contain the same number of unique named entities (7).

(g) They contain one foreign word: *Science* in *Star* and *Jean Gaudant* in *Fish*.

(h) They contain one number: *6.300 años luz* ('6,300 light years') in *Star* and *10 millones de años* ('10 millions of years') in *Fish*.

As seen in Figure 1, in variant A, text 2 includes a graphical scheme while text 1 was presented without the graphical scheme. Variant B is reversed: text 1 appeared with a graphical scheme and text 2 without it. The order of the experiments was counterbalanced using the variants A and B to guarantee that the participant never reads the same text twice.

For the layout of the texts and graphical schemes we chose a recommended font type for dyslexics, sans serif arial (Al-Wabil et al., 2007), unjustified text (Pedley, 2006), and recommended color and brightness contrast using a black font with creme background[1] (British Dyslexia Association, 2012).

For the creation of the graphical schemes[2] we took into account the pedagogical recommendations for dyslexics (Ramírez Sánchez, 2011; Chalkley et al., 2001), and the cognitive principles of inductive learning in concept acquisition from scheme theory (Anderson et al., 1979; Anderson and Robert, 2000). Since the tests were going to be read by dyslexics, the graphical schemes were manually created by a dyslexic adult and supervised by a psychologist. The graphical schemes simplify the discourse and highlight the most important information from the title and the content. Each of the graphical schemes shares the following pattern: the first line of the graphical scheme encloses the main words of the title connected by arrows and then, starting from the title, there is a node for each of the sentences of the text. These nodes summarize the most relevant information of the text, as the example translated to English shown in Figure 2. We present the original text and its translation in the Appendix.

To control the comprehension, after each text we designed a maximum performance questionnaire including inferential items related to the main idea. We did not include items related to details, because they involve memory more than comprehension (Sinatra et al., 1984). Each of the items had

[1]The CYMK are creme (FAFAC8) and black (000000). Color difference: 700, brightness difference: 244.

[2]Notice that we distinguish graphical schemes from conceptual graphs (Sowa, 1983) or semantic maps (Sinatra et al., 1984).

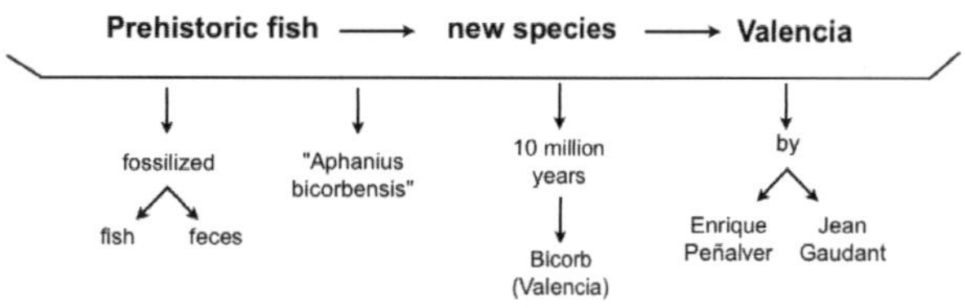

Figure 2: Example of a graphical scheme (*Fish*).

three answers, a correct one, another partially incorrect (normally containing details), and an incorrect one. We gave 100, 50, and 0 points for each type of answer, respectively. For instance (translated into English):

- What is the text about?
  (a) About the National Museum of Natural History in Paris (0 points).
  (b) About the discovery of a prehistoric fish in Valencia (100 points).
  (c) About the content of the fish feces (50 points).

The test finishes with one survey to learn the participant preferences. The survey is composed of three items about how helpful was the graphical scheme for (1) reading, (2) understanding, and (3) remembering the text. Each item uses a Likert scale with 5 levels, from strongly disagree (1) to strongly agree (5). An example of an item follows:

- Without the graphical scheme, my understanding of the text would have been:
  1. Much more easier because I did not understand anything about the graphical scheme.
  2. Easier because the graphical scheme is complicated.
  3. Neither easier nor more difficult.
  4. More difficult because the graphical scheme has helped me.
  5. Much more difficult because the graphical scheme has shed light about the content.

3.3 Equipment

The eye tracker used was a Tobii T50 (Tobii Technology, 2005) with a 17-inch TFT monitor. The eye tracker was calibrated for each participant and the light focus was always in the same position. The distance between the participant and the eye tracker was constant (approximately 60 cm. or 24 in.) and controlled by using a fixed chair.

3.4 Procedure

The sessions were conducted at Pompeu Fabra University and they took around 30 minutes, depending on the amount of information given by the participant. In each session the participant was alone with the interviewer (first author) in the quiet room prepared for the study.

The first part began with an interview designed to collect demographic information. Second, we proceeded with the recordings of the passages using eye tracking. Half of the participants made variant A of the test and the other half variant B. The participant was asked to read the texts in silence and completing each comprehension questionnaire. The text ends by answering the survey.

3.5 Data Analysis

The software used for analyzing the eye tracking data was Tobii Studio 3.0 and the R 2.14.1 statistical software. The measures used for the comparison of the text passages were the means of the fixation duration and the total duration of reading. Differences between groups and parameter values were tested by means of a one-way analysis of variance (ANOVA).

4 Results

In this section we present first the analyses of the data from the eye tracking and comprehension questionnaires (Section 4.1), followed by the analysis of the survey (Section 4.2).

4.1 Readability and Understandability

To measure the impact of graphical schemes in readability we analyzed the means of the fixation time and the total reading duration of the passages. Shorter fixations are preferred to longer ones because according to previous studies (Just and Carpenter, 1980), readers make longer fixations at points where processing loads are greater. Also, shorter reading durations are preferred to longer ones since faster reading is related to more readable texts (Williams et al., 2003). We compare readability with understandability through the inferential items of the comprehension questionnaire.

First, we studied the differences between the dyslexic participants and the control group. Then,

Table 1: Experimental results of the eye-tracking and the comprehension user study.

Measure (sec., %) (ave. $\pm$ std.dev.)	Scheme + Text	Text
	Group D	
Fixations Duration	0.224 ± 0.046	0.248 ± 0.057
Visit Duration	64.747 ± 22.469	78.493 ± 34.639
Correct Answers	86.93%	97.73%
	Group N	
Fixations Duration	0.205 ± 0.033	0.198 ± 0.030
Visit Duration	43.771 ± 14.790	45.124 ± 13.353
Correct Answers	89.58%	95.83%

we analyzed the influence of the graphical schemes in the readability and understandability.

In (Kurniawan and Conroy, 2006) it was found that students with dyslexia are not slower in reading than students without dyslexia when the articles are presented in a dyslexia friendly colour scheme. However, we found statistical significance among the dyslexic and non-dyslexic groups when reading both texts without graphical schemes taking into account the mean of fixation time ($p < 0.0008$) and the total reading duration for the texts with graphical schemes ($p < 0.0007$) and without graphical schemes ($p < 0.0001$) (see Table 1). On the other hand, our results are consistent with other eye-tracking studies to diagnose dyslexia that found statistical differences among the two populations (Eden et al., 1994).

The presence of graphical schemes improves the readability of the text for people with dyslexia because the fixation time and the reading duration decreases for all texts with a graphical scheme (see Tables 1, 2, and 3). Notice that these positive results are given for the comparison of the texts alone (see the text areas in Figure 1). If we compare the total reading duration of the text alone with the text plus the graphical scheme, it takes in average 18.6% more time to read the whole slide than the text alone.

However, we found no statistically significant results among texts with and without graphical schemes using such measures. The greatest difference in readability among texts with and without graphical schemes was found taking into account the fixation times for both texts ($p = 0.146$) among the dyslexic participants.

Comparing both *Fish* and *Star* texts (see Tables 2 and 3), we observe that *Fish* was more difficult to read and understand since it presents longer fixations and a lower rate of correct answers. In dyslexics the fixation time decreases more (from 0.258 seconds without graphical scheme to 0.227 with a graphical scheme, $p < 0.228$) in *Fish* that in *Star* (0.237 to 0.222, $p < 0.405$), meaning that graphical schemes have a higher impact in readability for complex texts.

Considering the similarity of the texts, it is surprising how *Fish* seems to be easier to read than *Star*. One possible explanation is that the scientific piece of news contained in *Star* was more present in the media than the other news contained in *Fish*.

However, graphical schemes have not helped our participants to increase their rate of correct answers for the inferential items. For all the cases except one (non-dyslexic participants in *Star*, Table 2) the rate of correct answers decreased when the text was accompanied by a scheme.

Dyslexic participants have a higher percentage of correct answers than non-dyslexics when the text is presented with the graphical scheme, and lower rate if the text is presented without the graphical scheme. These results are consistent with some of the opinions that the participants expressed after the session. A few dyslexic participants explained that the graphical scheme actually distracted them from the text content. Another dyslexic participant exposed that the graphical schemes helped her to remember and study texts but not to understand them. The diverse opinions of the participants towards the graphical schemes suggest that normally graphical schemes are highly customized by the person that creates them and therefore a non-customized schema could complicate understandability.

4.2 Survey

Through the user survey we infer how the participants were influenced by the graphical schemes in: (1) the text's readability, (2) the understandability of the text, and (3) remembering the text content. In Figure 3 we present the results for each of the items comparing dyslexic and non-dyslexic participants ($N = 23$).

In terms of readability, dyslexic and non-dyslexic participants have opposite opinions. While dyslexic participants agree in finding graphical schemes help-

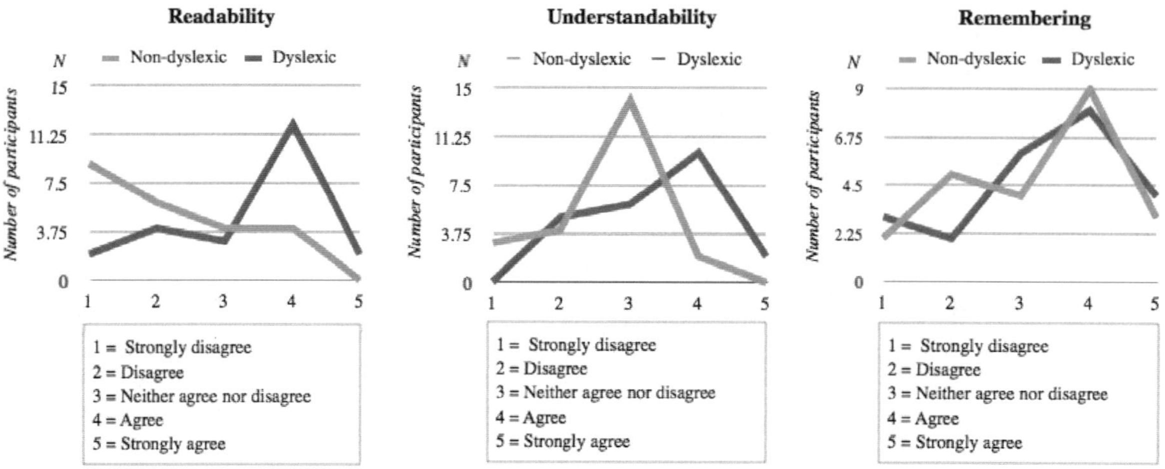

Figure 3: Survey results for understandability, readability and remembering.

Table 2: Experimental results of the eye-tracking and comprehension user study for text 1, *Star*.

Measure (sec., %) (ave. ± std.dev.)	Scheme + Text	Text
	Group D	
Fixations Duration	0.222 ± 0.061	0.237 ± 0.023
Visit Duration	63.633 ± 0.00	83.918 ± 18.606
Correct Answers	87.5%	95.45%
	Group N	
Fixations Duration	0.205 ± 0.023	0.199 ± 0.041
Visit Duration	39.552 ± 14.850	47.351 ± 15.580
Correct Answers	91.67%	91.67%

Table 3: Experimental results of the eye-tracking and comprehension user study for text 2, *Fish*.

Measure (sec., %) (ave. ± std.dev.)	Scheme + Text	Text
	Group D	
Fixations Duration	0.227 ± 0.026	0.258 ± 0.078
Visit Duration	60.073 ± 20.684	69.058 ± 29.910
Correct Answers	86.36%	100%
	Group N	
Fixations Duration	0.205 ± 0.042	0.214 ± 0.036
Visit Duration	47.990 ± 14.130	42.896 ± 10.991
Correct Answers	87.5%	100%

ful for reading (12 participants, 52.17%), non-dyslexic participants said that graphical schemes were unhelpful. Some participants explained that the graphical schemes mislead them because they were placed at the beginning of the slide when they did not know the topic of the text. However, a few participants claimed that they found the graphical schemes very helpful.

Participants with dyslexia mostly agree (10 participants, 43.48%) in finding graphical schemes helpful for textual comprehension while most of the non-dyslexic participants (14 participants, 60.87%) did not find graphical schemes neither helpful nor unhelpful for understandability. On the other hand, both populations agree in finding graphical schemes helpful for remembering data from the text.

5 Conclusions and Future Work

The addition of informational elements to a text impacts its readability. Since dyslexics are strong visual thinkers this study relates the use of graphical schemes to readability and understandability, contributing to predict their impact.

In general terms, we can affirm that adding a graphical scheme in a text improves its readability, since we observed a decrease in the fixation time and an increase of reading speed in texts containing graphical schemes. On the contrary to the expected result, understandability does not improve with the presence of graphical schemes.

Even though dyslexia presents heterogenous manifestations among subjects, we found patterns related to readability and understandability using quantitative and qualitative data.

However, our results shall be taken with care since readability, specially in dyslexic users, depends on many factors which are very challenging to control in an experimental setup. These factor include the vocabulary of the participants, their working memory or the different strategies they use to overcome dyslexia.

Further work is needed such as the inclusion of more types of graphical schemes in the experiments, the addition of a delayed post-test to address the effect of supplemental graphical schemes on robustness of learning, and the exploration of more factors related to readability.

Acknowledgments

We thank Mari-Carmen Marcos for her assistance with the eye tracker hardware and Joaquim Llisterri for his invaluable help distributing our experiments announcement among experts. Special thanks go for the psychologists Daniela Alarcón Sánchez and Clara María Pavón Gonzalo for their help when designing the questionnaires and graphical schemes. For their altruistic help in contacting dyslexic people we are indebted to Anna Eva Jarabo, María Fuentes Fort, Beatriu Pasarin, Dúnia Pèrdrix i Solàs, Toni Martí, Verónica Moreno, Emma Rodero, Olga Soler, Berta Torres, María Vilaseca, and Silvia Zaragoza. Special thanks go to all the anonymous dyslexic participants and their families. Finally, we thank the anonymous reviewers for their excellent comments.

References

A. Al-Wabil, P. Zaphiris, and S. Wilson. 2007. Web navigation for individuals with dyslexia: an exploratory study. *Universal Acess in Human Computer Interaction. Coping with Diversity*, pages 593–602.

J.R. Anderson and J. Robert. 2000. *Learning and memory*. John Wiley New York.

J.R. Anderson, P.J. Kline, and C.M. Beasley. 1979. A general learning theory and its application to schema abstraction. *Psychology of learning and motivation*, 13:277–318.

R. Barzilay, N. Elhadad, and K. R. McKeown. 2002. Inferring strategies for sentence ordering in multidocument news summarization. *Journal of Artificial Intelligence Research*, 17:35–55.

Stefan Bott and Horacio Saggion. 2012. Text simplification tools for spanish. In *Proceedings of the eighth international conference on Language Resources and Evaluation (LREC 2012)*, Instanbul, Turkey, May. ELRA.

British Dyslexia Association. 2012. Dyslexia style guide, January. `http://www.bdadyslexia.org.uk/`.

B. Chalkley, J. Waterfield, and Geography Discipline Network. 2001. *Providing learning support for students with hidden disabilities and dyslexia undertaking fieldwork and related activities*. University of Gloucestershire, Geography Discipline Network.

GF Eden, JF Stein, HM Wood, and FB Wood. 1994. Differences in eye movements and reading problems in dyslexic and normal children. *Vision Research*, 34(10):1345–1358.

J. Elkind, K. Cohen, and C. Murray. 1993. Using computer-based readers to improve reading comprehension of students with dyslexia. *Annals of Dyslexia*, 43(1):238–259.

Peter Gregor and Alan F. Newell. 2000. An empirical investigation of ways in which some of the problems encountered by some dyslexics may be alleviated using computer techniques. In *Proceedings of the fourth international ACM conference on Assistive technologies*, ASSETS 2000, pages 85–91, New York, NY, USA. ACM.

International Dyslexia Association. 2011. Definition of dyslexia: `http://interdys.org/DyslexiaDefinition.htm`. Based in the initial definition of the Research Committee of the Orton Dyslexia Society, former name of the IDA, done in 1994.

K. Inui, A. Fujita, T. Takahashi, R. Iida, and T. Iwakura. 2003. Text simplification for reading assistance: a project note. In *Proceedings of the second international workshop on Paraphrasing-Volume 16*, pages 9–16. Association for Computational Linguistics.

M.A. Just and P.A. Carpenter. 1980. A theory of reading: From eye fixations to comprehension. *Psychological review*, 87:329–354.

J. Kiraly and P.M. Ridge. 2001. Method of and apparatus for multi-modal information presentation to computer users with dyslexia, reading disabilities or visual impairment. US Patent 6,324,511.

A.W. Kotula. 2003. Matching readers to instructional materials: The use of classic readability measures for students with language learning disabilities and dyslexia. *Topics in Language Disorders*, 23(3):190.

S. Kurniawan and G. Conroy. 2006. Comparing comprehension speed and accuracy of online information in students with and without dyslexia. *Advances in Universal Web Design and Evaluation: Research, Trends and Opportunities, Idea Group Publishing, Hershey, PA*, pages 257–70.

M.R. López Castro. 2010. Intervención educativa en un caso real de problemas de comprensión lectora. *Hekademos: revista educativa digital*, (6):27–48.

K. Nandhini and SR Balasundaram. 2011. Improving readability of dyslexic learners through document summarization. In *IEEE International Conference on Technology for Education (T4E)*, pages 246–249. IEEE.

M. Pedley. 2006. Designing for dyslexics: Part 3 of 3. `http://accessites.org/site/2006/11/designing-for-dyslexics-part-3-of-3`.

D. M. Ramírez Sánchez. 2011. Estrategias de intervención educativa con el alumnado con dislexia. *Innovación y experiencias educativas*, 49.

L. Rello and R. Baeza-Yates. 2012. Lexical quality as a proxy for web text understandability (poster). In *The 21st International World Wide Web Conference (WWW 2012)*, April.

L. Rello, G. Kanvinde, and R. Baeza-Yates. 2012. Layout guidelines for web text and a web service to improve accessibility for dyslexics. In *International Cross Disciplinary Conference on Web Accessibility (W4A 2014)*, Lyon, France, April. ACM Press.

R.C. Sinatra, J. Stahl-Gemake, and D.N. Berg. 1984. Improving reading comprehension of disabled readers through semantic mapping. *The Reading Teacher*, 38(1):22–29.

L. Sitbon and P. Bellot. 2008. A readability measure for an information retrieval process adapted to dyslexics. In *Second international workshop on Adaptive Information Retrieval (AIR 2008 in conjunction with IIiX 2008)*, pages 52–57.

J.F. Sowa. 1983. *Conceptual structures: information processing in mind and machine*. Addison-Wesley Pub., Reading, MA.

Tobii Technology. 2005. Product description Tobii 50 Series.

F.R. Vellutino, J.M. Fletcher, M.J. Snowling, and D.M. Scanlon. 2004. Specific reading disability (dyslexia): What have we learned in the past four decades? *Journal of child psychology and psychiatry*, 45(1):2–40.

P.A. Weaver. 1978. Comprehension, recall, and dyslexia: A proposal for the application of schema theory. *Annals of Dyslexia*, 28(1):92–113.

T.G. West. 2009. *In the Mind's Eye: Creative Visual Thinkers, Gifted Dyslexics, and the Rise of Visual Technologies*. Prometheus Books.

S. Williams, E. Reiter, and L. Osman. 2003. Experiments with discourse-level choices and readability. In *Proceedings of the 9th European Workshop on Natural Language Generation (ENLG-2003)*, Budapest, Hungary.

A Appendix

Below we present Text 2 (*Fish*) and its translation to English.

Descubren en Valencia una nueva especie de pez prehistórico

El estudio de un lago salino que existió hace 10 millones de años en Bicorb (Valencia) ha permitido descubrir el fósil de una nueva especie de pez prehistórico y de sus heces. Según informó este martes el Instituto Geológico y Minero de España, este pez depredador ha sido bautizado por los investigadores como "Aphanius bicorbensis", en honor a la población de Bicorb donde ha sido encontrado. La investigacin ha sido realizada por Enrique Peñalver, experto en insectos fósiles del Instituto Geológico y Minero, y por Jean Gaudant, especialista en peces fósiles del Museo Nacional de Historia Natural de París, gracias a la financiación de la Consejería de Cultura de la Generalitat Valenciana. El estudio del contenido de las heces de estos peces, que también quedaron fosilizadas en la roca, ha permitido a los investigadores saber que este depredador se alimentaba de los foraminíferos y de las larvas de mosquito, especialmente abundantes en el lago.

A new species of a prehistoric fish is discovered in Valencia

The study of a saline lake that existed 10 million years ago in Bicorb (Valencia) has uncovered the fossil of a new species of prehistoric fish and their feces. The Geological and Mining Institute of Spain informed last Tuesday that this predatory fish has been named by the researchers as "Aphanius bicorbensis" in honor of the town of Bicorb where was found. The research was conducted by Enrique Peñalver, an expert on insect fossils of the Geological and Mining Institute, and Jean Gaudant, a specialist in fossil fishes of the National Museum of Natural History in Paris, thanks to funding from the Council of Culture of the Government of Valencia. The study of the content of the feces of these fishes, which were also fossilized in the rock, has allowed researchers to know that this predator was feeding on foraminifera and mosquito larvae, especially abundant in the lake.

Building Readability Lexicons with Unannotated Corpora

Julian Brooke* **Vivian Tsang†** **David Jacob†** **Fraser Shein*†** **Graeme Hirst***

*Department of Computer Science
University of Toronto
{jbrooke,gh}@cs.toronto.edu

†Quillsoft Ltd.
Toronto, Canada
{vtsang, djacob, fshein}@quillsoft.ca

Abstract

Lexicons of word difficulty are useful for various educational applications, including readability classification and text simplification. In this work, we explore automatic creation of these lexicons using methods which go beyond simple term frequency, but without relying on age-graded texts. In particular, we derive information for each word type from the readability of the web documents they appear in and the words they co-occur with, linearly combining these various features. We show the efficacy of this approach by comparing our lexicon with an existing coarse-grained, low-coverage resource and a new crowdsourced annotation.

1 Introduction

With its goal of identifying documents appropriate to readers of various proficiencies, automatic analysis of readability is typically approached as a text-level classification task. Although at least one popular readability metric (Dale and Chall, 1995) and a number of machine learning approaches to readability rely on lexical features (Si and Callan, 2001; Collins-Thompson and Callan, 2005; Heilman et al., 2007; Petersen and Ostendorf, 2009; Tanaka-Ishii et al., 2010), the readability of individual lexical items is not addressed directly in these approaches. Nevertheless, information about the difficulty of individual lexical items, in addition to being useful for text readability classification (Kidwell et al., 2009), can be applied to other tasks, for instance lexical simplification (Carroll et al., 1999; Burstein et al., 2007).

Our interest is in providing students with educational software that is sensitive to the difficulty of particular English expressions, providing proactive support for those which are likely to be outside a reader's vocabulary. However, our existing lexical resource is coarse-grained and lacks coverage. In this paper, we explore the extent to which an automatic approach could be used to fill in the gaps of our lexicon. Prior approaches have generally depended on some kind of age-graded corpus (Kidwell et al., 2009; Li and Feng, 2011), but this kind of resource is unlikely to provide the coverage that we require; instead, our methods here are based on statistics from a huge web corpus. We show that frequency, an obvious proxy for difficulty, is only the first step; in fact we can derive key information from the documents that words appear in and the words that they appear with, information that can be combined to give high performance in identifying relative difficulty. We compare our automated lexicon against our existing resource as well as a crowdsourced annotation.

2 Related Work

Simple metrics form the basis of much readability work: most involve linear combinations of word length, syllable count, and sentence length (Kincaid et al., 1975; Gunning, 1952), though the popular Dale-Chall reading score (Dale and Chall, 1995) is based on a list of 3000 'easy' words; a recent review suggests these metrics are fairly interchangeable (van Oosten et al., 2010). In machine-learning classification of texts by grade level, unigrams have been found to be reasonably effective for this task, outperforming readability metrics (Si and Callan, 2001; Collins-Thompson and Callan, 2005). Various other features have been explored, including parse (Petersen and Ostendorf, 2009) and coherence features (Feng et al., 2009), but the consensus seems to be that lexical features are the most consistently useful for automatic readability classification, even when considering non-native readers (Heilman et al., 2007).

In the field of readability, the work of Kidwell et al. (2009) is perhaps closest to ours. Like the above, their goal is text readability classification, but they proceed by first deriving an age of acquisition for each word based on its statistical distribution in age-annotated texts. Also similar is the work of Li and Feng (2011), who are critical of raw frequency as an indicator and instead identify core vocabulary based on the common use of words across different age groups. With respect to our goal of lowering reliance on fine-grained annotation, the work of Tanaka-Ishii et al. (2010) is also relevant; they create a readability system that requires only two general classes of text (easy and difficult), other texts are ranked relative to these two classes using regression.

Other lexical acquisition work has also informed our approach here. For instance, our co-occurrence method is an adaption of a technique applied in sentiment analysis (Turney and Littman, 2003), which has recently been shown to work for formality (Brooke et al., 2010), a dimension of stylistic variation that seems closely related to readability. Taboada et al. (2011) validate their sentiment lexicon using crowdsourced judgments of the relative polarity of pairs of words, and in fact crowd sourcing has been applied directly to the creation of emotion lexicons (Mohammad and Turney, 2010).

3 Resources

Our primary resource is an existing lexicon, previously built under the supervision of the one of authors. This resource, which we will refer to as the Difficulty lexicon, consists of 15,308 words and expressions classified into three difficulty categories: beginner, intermediate, and advanced. Beginner, which was intended to capture the vocabulary of early elementary school, is an amalgamation of various smaller sources, including the Dolch list (Dolch, 1948). The intermediate words, which include words learned in late elementary and middle school, were extracted from Internet-published texts written by students at these grade levels, and then filtered manually. The advanced words began as a list of common words that were in neither of the original two lists, but they have also been manually filtered; they are intended to reflect the vocabulary understood by the average high school student. Table 1 contains some examples from each list.

Table 1: Examples from the Difficulty lexicon

Beginner
coat, away, arrow, lizard, afternoon, rainy, carpet, earn, hear, chill
Intermediate
bale, campground, motto, intestine, survey, regularly, research, conflict
Advanced
contingency, scoff, characteristic, potent, myriad, detracted, illegitimate, overture

For our purposes here, we only use a subset of the Difficulty lexicon: we filtered out inflected forms, proper nouns, and words with non-alphabetic components (including multiword expressions) and then randomly selected 500 words from each level for our test set and 300 different words for our development/training set. Rather than trying to duplicate our arbitrary three-way distinction by manual or crowdsourced means, we instead focused on the relative difficulty of individual words: for each word in each of the two sets, we randomly selected three comparison words, one from each of the difficulty levels, forming a set of 4500 test pairs (2700 for the development set): $1/3$ of these pairs are words from the same difficulty level, $4/9$ are from adjacent difficulty levels, and the remaining $2/9$ are at opposite ends of our difficulty spectrum.

Our crowdsourced annotation was obtained using Crowdflower, which is an interface built on top of Mechanical Turk. For each word pair to be compared, we elicited 5 judgments from workers. Rather than frame the question in terms of difficulty or readability, which we felt was too subjective, we instead asked which of the two words the worker thought he or she learned first: the worker could choose either word, or answer "about the same time". They were instructed to choose the word they did know if one of the two words was unknown, and "same" if both were unknown. For our evaluation, we took the majority judgment as the gold standard; when there was no majority judgment, then the words were considered "the same". To increase the likelihood that our workers were native speakers of English, we required that the responses come from the US or Canada. Before running our main set, we ran several smaller test runs and manually inspected them for quality; although there were outliers, the majority of the judgments seemed reasonable.

Our corpus is the ICWSM Spinn3r 2009 dataset (Burton et al., 2009). We chose this corpus because it was used by Brooke et al. (2010) to derive a lexicon of formality; they found that it was more effective for these purposes than smaller mixed-register corpora like the BNC. The ICWSM 2009, collected over several weeks in 2008, contains about 7.5 million blogs, or 1.3 billion tokens, including well over a million word types (more than 200,000 of which which appear at least 10 times). We use only the documents which have at least 100 tokens. The corpus has been tagged using the TreeTagger (Schmid, 1995).

4 Automatic Lexicon Creation

Our method for lexicon creation involves first extracting a set of relevant numerical features for each word type. We can consider each feature as defining a lexicon on its own, which can be evaluated using our test set. Our features can be roughly broken into three types: simple features, document readability features, and co-occurrence features. The first of these types does not require much explanation: it includes the length of the word, measured in terms of letters and syllables (the latter is derived using a simple but reasonably accurate vowel-consonant heuristic), and the log frequency count in our corpus.[1]

The second feature type involves calculating simple readability metrics for each document in our corpus, and then defining the relevant feature for the word type as the average value of the metric for all the documents that the word appears in. For example, if D_w is the set of documents where word type w appears and d_i is the ith word in a document d, then the *document word length* (DWL) for w can be defined as follows:

$$DWL(w) = |D_w|^{-1} \sum_{d \in D_w} \frac{\sum_{i=0}^{|d|} length(d_i)}{|d|}$$

Other features calculated in this way include: the document sentence length, that is the average token length of sentences; the document type-token ratio[2]; and the document lexical density, the ratio of content words (nouns, verbs, adjectives, and adverbs) to all words.

The co-occurence features are inspired by the semi-supervised polarity lexicon creation method of Turney and Littman (2003). The first step is to build a matrix consisting of each word type and the documents it appears in; here, we use a binary representation, since the frequency with which a word appears in a particular document does not seem directly relevant to readability. We also do not remove traditional stopwords, since we believe that the use of certain common function words can in fact be good indicators of text readability. Once the matrix is built, we apply latent semantic analysis (Landauer and Dumais, 1997); we omit the mathematical details here, but the result is a dimensionality reduction such that each word is represented as a vector of some k dimensions. Next, we select two sets of seed words (P and N) which will represent the ends of the spectrum which we are interested in deriving. We derive a feature value V for each word by summing the cosine similarity of the word vector with all the seeds:

$$V(\mathbf{w}) = \frac{\sum_{\mathbf{p} \in P} \cos(\theta(\mathbf{w},\mathbf{p}))}{|P|} - \frac{\sum_{\mathbf{n} \in N} \cos(\theta(\mathbf{w},\mathbf{n}))}{|N|}$$

We further normalize this to a range of 1 to -1, centered around the core vocabulary word *and*. Here, we try three possible versions of P and N: the first, Formality, is the set of words used by Brooke et al. (2010) in their study of formality, that is, a

[1] Though it is irrelevant when evaluating the feature alone, the log frequency was noticeably better when combining frequency with other features.

[2] We calculate this using only the first 100 words of the document, to avoid the well-documented influence of length on TTR.

set of slang and other markers of oral communication as *N*, and a set of formal discourse markers and adverbs as *P*, with about 100 of each. The second, Childish, is a set of 10 common 'childish' concrete words (e.g. *mommy*, *puppy*) as *N*, and a set of 10 common abstract words (e.g. *concept*, *philosophy*) as *P*. The third, Difficulty, consists of the 300 beginner words from our development set as *N*, and the 300 advanced words from our development set as *P*. We tested several values of *k* for each of the seed sets (from 20 to 500); there was only small variation so here we just present our best results for each set as determined by testing in the development set.

Our final lexicon is created by taking a linear combination of the various features. We can find an appropriate weighting of each term by taking them from a model built using our development set. We test two versions of this: by default, we use a linear regression model where for training beginner words are tagged as 0, advanced words as 1, and intermediate words as 0.5. The second model is a binary SVM classifier; the features of the model are the difference between the respective features for each of the two words, and the classifier predicts whether the first or second word is more difficult. Both models were built using WEKA (Witten and Frank, 2005), with default settings except for feature normalization, which must be disabled in the SVM to get useful weights for the linear combination which creates our lexicon. In practice, we would further normalize our lexicon; here, however, this normalization is not relevant since our evaluation is based entirely on relative judgments. We also tested a range of other machine learning algorithms available in WEKA (e.g. decision trees and MaxEnt) but the crossvalidated accuracy was similar to or slightly lower than using a linear classifier.

5 Evaluation

All results are based on comparing the relative difficulty judgments made for the word pairs in our test set (or, more often, some subset) by the various sources. Since even the existing Difficulty lexicon is not entirely reliable, we report agreement rather than accuracy. Except for agreement of Crowdflower workers, agreement is the percentage of pairs where the sources agreed as compared to the total number of pairs. For agreement between Crowdflower workers, we follow Taboada et al. (2011) in calculating agreement across all possible pairings of each worker for each pair. Although we considered using a more complex metric such as Kappa, we believe that simple pairwise agreement is in fact equally interpretable when the main interest is relative agreement of various methods; besides, Kappa is intended for use with individual annotators with particular biases, an assumption which does not hold here.

To evaluate the reliability of our human-annotated resources, we look first at the agreement within the Crowdflower data, and between the Crowdflower and our Difficulty lexicon, with particular attention to within-class judgments. We then compare the predictions of various automatically extracted features and feature combinations with these human judgments; since most of these involve a continuous scale, we focus only on words which were judged to be different.[3] For the Difficulty lexicon (Diff.), the *n* in this comparison is 3000, while for the Crowdflower (CF) judgments it is 4002.

6 Results

We expect a certain amount of noise using crowdsourced data, and indeed agreement among Crowdflower workers was not extremely high, only 56.6% for a three-way choice; note, however, that in these circumstances a single worker disagreeing with the rest will drop pairwise agreement in that judgement to 60%.[4] Tellingly, average agreement was relatively high (72.5%) for words on the extremes of our difficulty spectrum, and low for words in the same difficulty category (46.0%), which is what we would expect. As noted by Taboada et al. (2011), when faced with a pairwise comparison task, workers tend to avoid the "same" option; instead, the proximity of the words on the underlying spectrum is reflected in disagreement. When we compare the crowdsourced judgements directly to the Difficulty lexicon, base

[3]A continuous scale will nearly always predict some difference between two words. An obvious approach would be to set a threshold within which two words will be judged the same, but the specific values depend greatly on the scale and for simplicity we do not address this problem here.

[4]In 87.3% of cases, at least 3 workers agreed; in 56.2% of cases, 4 workers agreed, and in 23.1% of cases all 5 workers agreed.

agreement is 63.1%. This is much higher than chance, but lower than we would like, considering these are two human-annotated sources. However, it is clear that much of this disagreement is due to "same" judgments, which are three times more common in the Difficulty lexicon-based judgments than in the Crowdflower judgments (even when disagreement is interpreted as a "same" judgment). Pairwise agreement of non-"same" judgments for word pairs which are in the same category in the Difficultly lexicon is high enough (45.9%)[5] for us to conclude that this is not random variation, strongly suggesting that there are important distinctions within our difficulty categories, i.e. that it is not sufficiently fine-grained. If we disregard all words that are judged as same in one (or both) of the two sources, the agreement of the resulting word pairs is 91.0%, which is reasonably high.

Table 2 contains the agreement when feature values or a linear combination of feature values are used to predict the readability of the unequal pairs from the two manual sources. First, we notice that the Crowdflower set is obviously more difficult, probably because it contains more pairs with fairly subtle (though noticeable) distinctions. Other clear differences between the annotations: whereas for Crowdflower frequency is the key indicator, this is not true for our original annotation, which prefers the more complex features we have introduced here. A few features did poorly in general: syllable count appears too coarse-grained to be useful on its own, lexical density is only just better than chance, and type-token ratio performs at or below chance. Otherwise, many of the features within our major types give roughly the same performance individually.

When we combine features, we find that simple and document features combine to positive effect, but the co-occurrence features are redundant with each other and, for the most part, the document features. A major boost comes, however, from combining either document or co-occurrence features with the simple features; this is especially true for our Difficulty lexicon annotation, where the gain is 7% to 8 percentage points. It does not seem to matter very much whether the weights of each feature are determined by pairwise classifier or by linear regression: this is interesting because it means we can train a model to create a readability spectrum with only pairwise judgments. Finally, we took all the 2500 instances where our two annotations agreed that one word was more difficult, and tested our best model against only those pairs. Results using this selective test set were, unsurprisingly, higher than those of either of the annotations alone: 91.2%, which is roughly the same as the original agreement between the two manual annotations.

[5]Random agreement here is 33.3%.

Table 2: Agreement (%) of automated methods with manual resources on pairwise comparison task (Diff. = Difficulty lexicon, CF = Crowdflower)

Features	**Resource**	
	Diff.	CF
Simple		
Syllable length	62.5	54.9
Word length	68.8	62.4
Term frequency	69.2	70.7
Document		
Avg. word length	74.5	66.8
Avg. sentence length	73.5	65.9
Avg. type-token ratio	47.0	50.0
Avg. lexical density	56.1	54.7
Co-occurrence		
Formality	74.7	66.5
Childish	74.2	65.5
Difficulty	75.7	66.1
Linear Combinations		
Simple	79.3	75.0
Document	80.1	70.8
Co-occurrence	76.0	67.0
Document+Co-occurrence	80.4	70.2
Simple+Document	87.5	79.1
Simple+Co-occurrence	86.7	78.2
All	**87.6**	**79.5**
All (SVM)	87.1	79.2

7 Discussion

Word difficulty is a vague concept, and we have admittedly sidestepped a proper definition here: instead, we hope to establish a measure of reliability in judgments of 'lexical readability' by looking for agreement across diverse sources of information. Our comparison of our existing resources with crowdsourced judgments suggests that some consistency is possible, but that granularity is, as we predicted, a serious concern, one which ultimately undermines our validation to some degree. An automatically derived lexicon, which can be fully continuous or as coarse-grained as needed, seems like an ideal solution, though the much lower performance of the automatic lexicon in predicting the more fine-grained Crowdflower judgments indicates that automatically-derived features are limited in their ability to deal with subtle differences. However, a visual inspection of the spectrum created by the automatic methods suggests that, with a judicious choice of granularity, it should be sufficient for our needs. In future work, we also intend to evaluate its use for readability classification, and perhaps expand it to include multiword expressions and syntactic patterns.

Our results clearly show the benefit of combining multiple sources of information to build a model of word difficulty. Word frequency and word length are of course relevant, and the utility of the document context features is not surprising, since they are merely a novel extension of existing proxies for readability. The co-occurrence features were also useful, though they seem fairly redundant and slightly inferior to document features; we posit that these features, in addition to capturing notions of register such as formality, may also offer semantic distinctions relevant to the acquisition process. For instance, children may have a large vocabulary in very concrete domains such as animals, including words (e.g. *lizard*) that are not particularly frequent in adult corpora, while very common words in other domains (such as the legal domain) are completely outside the range of their experience. If we look at some of the examples which term frequency alone does not predict, they seem to be very much of this sort: *dollhouse/emergence*, *skirt/industry*, *magic/system*. Unsupervised techniques for identifying semantic variation, such as LSA, can capture these sorts of distinctions. However, our results indicate that simply looking at the readability of the texts that these sort of words appear in (i.e. our document features) is mostly sufficient, and less than 10% of the pairs which are correctly ordered by these two feature sets are different. In any case, an age-graded corpus is definitely not required.

There are a few other benefits of using word co-occurrence that we would like to touch on, though we leave a full exploration for future work. First, if we consider readability in other languages, each language may have different properties which render proxies such as word length much less useful (e.g. ideographic languages like Chinese or agglutinative languages like Turkish). However, word (or lemma) co-occurrence, like frequency, is essentially a universal feature across languages, and thus can be directly extended to any language. Second, if we consider how we would extend difficulty-lexicon creation to the context of adult second-language learners, it might be enough to adjust our seed terms to reflect the differences in the language exposure of this population, i.e. we would expect difficulty in acquiring colloquialisms that are typically learned in childhood but are not part of the core vocabulary of the adult language.

8 Conclusion

In this paper, we have presented an automatic method for the derivation of a readability lexicon relying only on an unannotated word corpus. Our results show that although term frequency is a key feature, there are other, more complex features which provide competitive results on their own as well as combining with term frequency to improve agreement with manual resources that reflect word difficulty or age of acquisition. By comparing our manual lexicon with a new crowdsourced annotation, we also provide a validation of the resource, while at the same time highlighting a known issue, the lack of fine-grainedness. Our manual lexicon provides a solution for this problem, albeit at the cost of some reliability. Although our immediate interest is not text readability classification, the information derived could be applied fairly directly to this task, and might be particularly useful in the case when annotated texts are not avaliable.

Acknowledgments

This work was financially supported by the Natural Sciences and Engineering Research Council of Canada.

References

Julian Brooke, Tong Wang, and Graeme Hirst. 2010. Automatic acquisition of lexical formality. In *Proceedings of the 23rd International Conference on Computational Linguistics (COLING '10)*.

Jill Burstein, Jane Shore, John Sabatini, Yong-Won Lee, and Matthew Ventura. 2007. The automated text adaptation tool. In *Proceedings of the Annual Conference of the North American Chapter of the Association for Computational Linguistics (NAACL '07), Software Demonstrations*, pages 3–4.

Kevin Burton, Akshay Java, and Ian Soboroff. 2009. The ICWSM 2009 Spinn3r Dataset. In *Proceedings of the Third Annual Conference on Weblogs and Social Media (ICWSM 2009)*, San Jose, CA.

John Carroll, Guido Minnen, Darren Pearce, Yvonne Canning, Siobhan Devlin, and John Tait. 1999. Simplifying English text for language impaired readers. In *Proceedings of the 9th Conference of the European Chapter of the Association for Computational Linguistics (EACL'99)*, pages 269–270.

Kevyn Collins-Thompson and Jamie Callan. 2005. Predicting reading difficulty with statistical language models. *Journal of the American Society for Information Science Technology*, 56(13):1448–1462.

Edgar Dale and Jeanne Chall. 1995. *Readability Revisited: The New Dale-Chall Readability Formula*. Brookline Books, Cambridge, MA.

Edward William Dolch. 1948. *Problems in Reading*. The Garrard Press.

Lijun Feng, Noémie Elhadad, and Matt Huenerfauth. 2009. Cognitively motivated features for readability assessment. In *Proceedings of the 12th Conference of the European Chapter of the Association for Computational Linguistics (EACL '09)*, pages 229–237.

Robert Gunning. 1952. *The Technique of Clear Writing*. McGraw-Hill.

Michael J. Heilman, Kevyn Collins, and Jamie Callan. 2007. Combining lexical and grammatical features to improve readability measures for first and second language texts. In *Proceedings of the Conference of the North American Chapter of Association for Computational Linguistics (NAACL-HLT '07)*.

Paul Kidwell, Guy Lebanon, and Kevyn Collins-Thompson. 2009. Statistical estimation of word acquisition with application to readability prediction. In *Proceedings of the 2009 Conference on Empirical Methods in Natural Language Processing (EMNLP'09)*, pages 900–909.

J. Peter Kincaid, Robert. P. Fishburne Jr., Richard L. Rogers, and Brad. S. Chissom. 1975. Derivation of new readability formulas for Navy enlisted personnel. Research Branch Report 8-75, Millington, TN: Naval Technical Training, U. S. Naval Air Station, Memphis, TN.

Thomas K. Landauer and Susan Dumais. 1997. A solution to Plato's problem: The latent semantic analysis theory of the acquisition, induction, and representation of knowledge. *Psychological Review*, 104:211–240.

Hanhong Li and Alex C. Feng. 2011. Age tagging and word frequency for learners' dictionaries. In Harald Baayan John Newman and Sally Rice, editors, *Corpus-based Studies in Language Use, Language Learning, and Language Documentation*. Rodopi.

Saif Mohammad and Peter Turney. 2010. Emotions evoked by common words and phrases: Using Mechanical Turk to create an emotion lexicon. In *Proceedings of the NAACL HLT 2010 Workshop on Computational Approaches to Analysis and Generation of Emotion in Text*, pages 26–34, Los Angeles.

Sarah E. Petersen and Mari Ostendorf. 2009. A machine learning approach to reading level assessment. *Computer Speech and Language*, 23(1):89–106.

Helmut Schmid. 1995. Improvements in part-of-speech tagging with an application to German. In *Proceedings of the ACL SIGDAT Workshop*, pages 47–50.

Luo Si and Jamie Callan. 2001. A statistical model for scientific readability. In *Proceedings of the Tenth International Conference on Information and Knowledge Management (CIKM '01)*, pages 574–576.

Maite Taboada, Julian Brooke, Milan Tofiloski, Kimberly Voll, and Manifred Stede. 2011. Lexicon-based methods for sentiment analysis. *Computational Linguistics*, 37(2):267–307.

Kumiko Tanaka-Ishii, Satoshi Tezuka, and Hiroshi Terada. 2010. Sorting texts by readability. *Computational Linguistics*, 36(2):203–227.

Peter Turney and Michael Littman. 2003. Measuring praise and criticism: Inference of semantic orientation from association. *ACM Transactions on Information Systems*, 21:315–346.

Philip van Oosten, Dries Tanghe, and Veronique Hoste. 2010. Towards an improved methodology for automated readability prediction. In *Proceedings of the 7th International Conference on Language Resources and Evaluation (LREC '10)*.

Ian H. Witten and Eibe Frank. 2005. *Data Mining: Practical Machine Learning Tools and Techniques*. Morgan Kaufmann, San Francisco.

Making Readability Indices Readable

Sara Tonelli
FBK, Trento, Italy
satonelli@fbk.eu

Ke Tran Manh
Charles University, Prague, CR
ketranmanh@gmail.com

Emanuele Pianta
FBK, Trento, Italy
pianta@fbk.eu

Abstract

Although many approaches have been presented to compute and predict readability of documents in different languages, the information provided by readability systems often fail to show in a clear and understandable way how difficult a document is and which aspects contribute to content readability. We address this issue by presenting a system that, for a given document in Italian, provides not only a list of readability indices inspired by Coh-Metrix, but also a graphical representation of the difficulty of the text compared to the three levels of Italian compulsory education, namely elementary, middle and high-school level. We believe that this kind of representation makes readability assessment more intuitive, especially for educators who may not be familiar with readability predictions via supervised classification. In addition, we present the first available system for readability assessment of Italian inspired by Coh-Metrix.

1 Introduction

The task of readability assessment consists in quantifying how difficult a text is for a reader. This kind of assessment has been widely used for several purposes, such as evaluating the reading level of children and impaired persons and improving Web content accessibility for users with low literacy level.

While indices and methodologies for readability assessment of English have been widely investigated, and research on English readability has been continuously progressing thanks to advances in psycholinguistic research and in natural language processing, only limited efforts have been made to extend current approaches to other languages. An adaptation of the basic Flesch Index (Flesch, 1946) exists for many languages, but only in few cases more sophisticated approaches have been adopted, taking into account recent studies on text cohesion, readability and simplification.

With this work, we aim at bridging the gap between the standard approach to Italian readability based on the Gulpease index (following the same criteria of the Flesch Index) and the more advanced approaches to readability currently available for English and based on psycholinguistic principles. In particular, we present a set of indices for Italian readability covering different linguistics aspects, from the lexical to the discourse level, which are inspired by Coh-Metrix (Graesser et al., 2004). We make this analysis available online, but we differentiate our service from that of Coh-Metrix[1] in that we provide a graphical representation of the aspects affecting readability, comparing a document with the average indices of elementary, middle and high-school level texts. This makes readability analysis really intuitive, so that a user can straightforwardly understand how difficult a document is, and see if some aspects (e.g. lexicon, syntax, discourse) affect readability more than others.

Our research goals are: *i)* to analyze the adequacy of the Gulpease index for discriminating between the readability levels of texts used for teaching and testing in the Italian school practice, *ii)* to implement an adaptation of Coh-Metrix indices for Italian, *iii)* to make the readability analysis available online and

[1] http://cohmetrix.memphis.edu

understandable to naive users.

2 Related work

The first formulas to automatically compute the difficulty of a text were devised for English, starting from the Flesch Index (Flesch, 1946), followed by the Gunning Fog (Gunning, 1952), the SMOG index (McLaughlin, 1969) and the Fleisch-Kincaid (Kincaid et al., 1975). These metrics combine factors, such as word and sentence length, that are easy to compute and that should approximate the linguistic elements that impact on readability. Similar indexes have been proposed also for other languages such as German (Bamberger and Vanecek, 1984), French (Kandel and Moles, 1958) and Spanish (Huerta, 1959).

The first readability formula for Italian, the Flesch-Vacca (Franchina and Vacca, 1986), was introduced in the early seventies and was based on an adaptation of the Flesch index (Flesch, 1946). However, it has been widely replaced by the Gulpease index (Lucisano and Piemontese, 1988), which was introduced in the eighties by the Gruppo Universitario Linguistico Pedagogico (GULP) of the University of Rome. The Gulpease index takes into account the length of a word in characters rather than in syllables, which proved to be more reliable for assessing the readability of Italian texts. The index ranges from 0 (lowest readability) to 100 (maximum readability).

In recent years, research on English readability has progressed toward more sophisticated models that take into account difficulty at syntactic, semantic and discourse level thanks to advances in psycholinguistic accounts of text processing (Graesser et al., 2004) and to the availability of a wide range of NPL tools (e.g. dependency and constituency parsers, anaphora resolution systems, etc.) and resources (e.g. WordNet). However, for many other languages current approaches for readability assessment still rely on few basic factors. A notable exception is the Coh-Metrix-PORT tool (Scarton et al., 2009; Aluisio et al., 2010), which includes 60 readability measures for Brazilian Portuguese inspired by the Coh-Metrix (Graesser et al., 2004).

A different approach has been followed by the developers of the DeLite system for German (Glöckner et al., 2006; von der Brück et al., 2008): the tool computes a set of indices measuring the linguistic complexity of a document through deep parsing and outputs a final readability score obtained by applying the k-nearest neighbor algorithm based on 3,000 ratings from 300 users.

As for Italian, the only work aimed at improving on the performance of standard readability indices has been proposed by Dell'Orletta et al. (2011), who implement a set of lexical and morpho-syntactic features to distinguish between normal and simplified newspaper articles in a binary classification task. Our work differs from their approach in that we choose a different type of corpus for a different audience (i.e. children with different proficiency levels vs. adults with low literacy skills or mild cognitive impairment). We also enrich their feature set in that our indices capture also semantic and discourse aspects of a text. In this respect, we take advantage of cognitive and psycholinguistic evidence supporting the idea behind Coh-Metrix that high textual coherence and cohesion result in improved readability with any type of readers (Beck et al., 1984s; Cataldo and Oakhill, 2000; Linderholm et al., 2000), and that discourse connectives and spatio-temporal information in a text strongly contribute to cohesion.

3 The corpus

Our goal is to develop a system that can be used in real scenarios, for instance by teachers who want to assess if a text is understandable by children in a certain class. Therefore, we avoid collecting a corpus with documents showing different degrees of simplification according to a 'controlled' scenario. This strategy was adopted for instance by Crossley et al. (2011), who compared different readability indices using news texts manually simplified into advanced, intermediate and beginning difficulty level. Also the experiments on readability assessment of Portuguese texts by Scarton et al. (2009) were conducted on a corpus of news articles manually simplified by a linguist according to a natural and a strong simplification level.

Our approach is different in that we take texts used for teaching and comprehension exercises in Italian schools and divide them into three classes, according to the class level in which they are em-

	Class 1 (63 docs)	**Class 2** (55 docs)	**Class 3** (62 docs)
Doc. length in tokens	530 (± 273)	776 (± 758)	1085 (± 1152)
Gulpease	55.92 (± 6.35)	53.88 (± 6.13)	50.54 (± 6.98)

Table 1: Corpus statistics. All values are averaged. StDev is reported between parenthesis.

ployed. This means that in Class 1 we collect all documents written for children in elementary schools (aged 6-10), in Class 2 we collect texts for children in middle schools (aged 11-13), and in Class 3 we gather documents written for teenagers in high schools (aged 14-18). The classes contain respectively 63, 55 and 62 documents.

As shown in Table 1, the average length of the documents increases with the school level. However, the single documents show high variability, especially those in Class 3. Texts have been selected so as to represent the most common genres and knowledge domains in school texts. Thus, the corpus contains a balanced selection of both narrative and expository texts. The latter belong mostly to the following domains: history, literature, biology, physics, chemistry, geography and philosophy. The corpus includes also all official text comprehension tests used in Italy in the INVALSI school proficiency evaluation campaign[2].

4 Readability assessment based on Gulpease

We first analyze the behaviour of the Gulpease index in our corpus, in order to assess if this measure is adequate for capturing the readability of the documents. We compute the index by applying to each document the standard formula:

$$Gulp_{doc} = 89 + \frac{(300 * \#sents_{doc}) - (10 * \#chars_{doc})}{\#tokens_{doc}}$$

Average Gulpease and standard deviation for each class are reported in Table 1.

[2]National Institute for the Evaluation of the Educational System by the Ministry of Research and University, http://www.invalsi.it/invalsi/index.php

Fig. 1 shows the distribution of the Gulpease index in the corpus. On the x axis the document id is reported, with document 1–63 belonging to Class 1 (elementary), document 64–118 to Class 2 (middle) and 119–180 to Class 3 (high school). On the y axis, the Gulpease index is reported, ranging from 41 (i.e. the lowest readability level in the corpus) to 87 (i.e. highest readability).

Although the highest readability score is obtained by a document of Class 1, and the lowest scores concern documents in Class 3, the three classes do not seem to be separable based solely on Gulpease. In particular, documents in Class 2, written for students in middle school, show scores partly overlapping with Class 1 and partly with Class 3. Furthermore, the great majority of the documents in the corpus have a Gulpease index included between 50 and 60 and the average Gulpease does not differ consistently across the three classes (Table 1).

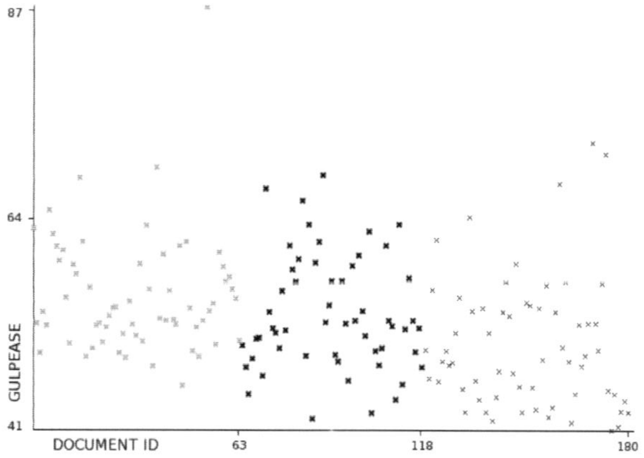

Figure 1: Distribution of Gulpease index in the corpus. Document id on x axis, and Gulpease on y axis

For children in the elementary school, a text with a Gulpease index between 0 and 55 usually corresponds to the frustration level. For children in the middle school, the frustration level is reached with a Gulpease index between 0 and 35. For high-school students, this level is reached with Gulpease being between 0 and 10.[3]

[3]More information on how to interpret Gulpease for each of the three classes is reported at http://www.eulogos.net/ActionPagina_1045.do

4.1 Coh-Metrix for English

Coh-Metrix is a computational tool available online at http://cohmetrix.memphis.edu that can analyze an English document and produce a list of indices expressing the cohesion of the text. These indices have been devised based on psycholinguistic studies on the mental representation of textual content (McNamara et al., 1996) and address various characteristics of explicit text, from lexicon to syntax, semantics and discourse, that contribute to the creation of this representation. Although the tool relies on widely used NLP techniques such as PoS tagging and parsing, there have been limited attempts to employ it in studies on automatic assessment of text cohesion. Nevertheless, recent works in the NLP community investigating the impact of entity grids (Barzilay and Lapata, 2008) or of discourse relations (Pitler and Nenkova, 2008) on text coherence and readability go in the same direction as research on Coh-Metrix, in that they aim at identifying the linguistic features that best express readability at syntactic, semantic and discourse level.

The indices belonging to Coh-Metrix are divided into five main classes:

- *General Word and Text Information*: The indices in this class capture the correlation between brain's processing time and word-level information. For example, many syllables in a word or many words in a sentence are likely to make a document more difficult for the brain to process it. Also, if the type/token ratio is high, the text should be more difficult because there are many unique words to be decoded.
- *Syntactic Indices*: The indices in this class assess syntactic complexity and the frequency of particular syntactic constituents in a text. The intuition behind this class is that high syntactic complexity makes a text more difficult to process, lowering its readability, because it usually implies syntactic ambiguity, structural density, high number of embedded constituents.
- *Referential and Semantic Indices*: These indices assess the negative impact on readability of cohesion gaps, which occur when the words in a sentence do not connect to other sentences in the text. They are based on coreference and anaphoric chains as well as on semantic similarity between segments of the same document exploiting Latent Semantic Analysis (LSA).
- *Indices for Situation Model Dimensions*: The indices in this class express the degree of complexity of the mental model evoked by a document (Dijk and Kintsch, 1983) and involves four main dimensions: causality, intentionality, time and space.
- *Standard readability indices*: They comprise traditional indices for readability assessment including Flesch Reading Ease and Flesch Kincaid Grade Level.

Although the developers of Coh-Metrix claim that the internal version of the tool includes hundreds of measures, the online demo shows only 60 of them. This is partly due to the fact that some metrics are computed using resources protected by copyright, and partly because the whole framework is still under development. We refer to these 60 metrics in order to implement the Coh-Metrix version for Italian, that we call *Coease*.

4.2 *Coease*: Coh-Metrix for Italian

In the Coh-Metrix adaptation for Italian, we follow as much as possible the description of the single indices reported on the official Coh-Metrix documentation. However, in some cases, not all implementation details are given, so that we may have slightly different versions of single indices. Besides, one set of indices is based on the MRC Psycholinguistic Database (Wilson, 2003), a resource including around 150,000 words with concreteness ratings collected through psycholinguistic experiments, which is not available for Italian. In general terms, however, we try to have some indices for each of the classes described in Section 4.1, in order to represent all relevant aspects of text cohesion.

The list of all indices is reported in Table 2. Indices from 1 to 6 capture some information about the length of the documents in terms of syllables, words, sentences and paragraphs. Syllables are computed using the Perl module Lingua::IT::Hyphenate[4].

[4] http://search.cpan.org/~acalpini/Lingua-IT-Hyphenate-0.14/

Indices from 7 to 10 focus on *familiarity* of content words (verbs, nouns, adjectives and adverbs) measured as their frequency in a reference corpus. While in English the frequency list was the CELEX database (Baayen et al., 1995), for Italian we extracted it from the dump of Italian Wikipedia[5]. The idea behind these indices is that unfamiliar words or technical terminology should have a low frequency in the reference corpus, which is supposed to be a general corpus representing many domains. Index 8 is the logarithm of raw frequency of content words, because logarithm proved to be compatible with reading time (Haberlandt and Graesser, 1985). Index 9 is obtained by computing first the lowest frequency score among all the content words in each sentence, and then calculating the mean. Index 10 is obtained by computing first the lowest log frequency score among all content words in each sentence, and then calculating the mean. Content words were extracted by running the TextPro NLP suite for Italian (Pianta et al., 2008)[6] and keeping only words tagged with one of WordNet PoS, namely *v*, *a*, *n* and *r*.

Indices 11 and 12 compute the *abstractness* of nouns and verbs by measuring the distance between the WordNet synset containing the lemma (most frequent sense) and the root. Then, the mean distance of all nouns and verbs in the text is computed. We obtain this index using MultiWordNet (Pianta et al., 2002), the Italian version of WordNet, aligned at synset level with the English one.

Indices from 13 to 17 measure the *syntactic complexity* of sentences based on parsing output. Indices 13-15 are computed after parsing each sentence with the Italian version of Berkeley constituency-based parser (Lavelli and Corazza, 2009)[7]. *NP incidence* is the incidence of atomic NPs (i.e. not containing any other NPs) per 1000 words. *Higher-level constituents* index is the mean distance between each terminal word in the text and the parse tree root. *Main verb information* needed for computing index 16 is obtained by parsing each sentence with Malt parser for Italian (Lavelli et al., 2009) and taking the sentence root as main verb. The index accounts for the memory load needed by a reader to understand a sentence. Index 17 is calculated by comparing each token to a manual list of negations and computing the *total number of negations per 1000 words*.

Indices 18 and 19 are computed again using TextPro and the output of Berkeley parser. Index 18 is the ratio of words labelled as *pronouns* to the incidence of all NPs in the text. High pronoun density implies low readability, because it makes referential cohesion less explicit.

Indices from 20 to 29 capture the cohesion of sentences by taking into account different types of connectives. In order to compute them, we manually create lists of connectives divided into *additive*, *causal*, *logical* and *temporal*. Then, for each list, we identify positive (i.e. extending events) and negative (i.e. ceasing to extend expected events) connectives. For instance, 'inoltre' ('moreover') is a positive additive connective, while 'ma' ('but') is a negative additive connective. We further compute the incidence of conditional operators by comparing each token to a manual list. In order to create such lists, we stick to their English version by first translating them into Italian and then manually adding some missing connectives. However, this does not avoid ambiguity, since some connectives with high frequency can appear in more than one list, for instance 'e' ('and'), which can be both temporal and additive.

Indices 30 and 31 capture *syntactic similarity* of sentences and are based on the assumption that a document showing high syntactic variability is more difficult to understand. This index computes the proportion of intersecting nodes between two syntactic trees by looking for the largest common subtree, so that every node except terminal node has the same production rule in both trees. Index 32 calculates the proportion of adjacent sentences that *share at least one argument* expressed by a noun or a pronoun, while indices 33 and 34 compute this proportion based on stems and content words. Stems are obtained by applying the Snowball stemmer[8] to the lemmatized documents.

Indices 35–40 capture the situation model dimensions of the text. *Causal and intentional cohesion* corresponds to the ratio between causal or intentional particles (i.e. connectives and adverbs) and

[5] http://it.wikipedia.org

[6] TextPro achieved 95% PoS tagging accuracy at Evalita 2009 evaluation campaign for Italian tools.

[7] The parser achieved 84% F1 at Evalita 2011 evaluation campaign for Italian tools.

[8] http://snowball.tartarus.org/

causal or intentional verbs. The rationale behind this is that a text with many causal verbs and few causal particles is less readable because the connections between events is not explicitly expressed. Since no details where given on how these particles and verbs were extracted for English, we devise our own methodology. First, we produce manual lists of causal and intentional particles in Italian. As for *causal* verbs, we first select all synsets in the English WordNet containing 'cause to' in their glosses, and then obtain the corresponding version in Italian through MultiWordNet. *Intentional* verbs are obtained by first extracting all verbs from English WordNet that belong to the following categories: cognition, communication, competition, consumption, contact, creation, emotion, motion and perception, and then mapping them to the Italian corresponding verbs in MultiWordNet. *Temporal* cohesion is computed as the average of repetitions of tense and aspect in the document. Repetitions are calculated by mapping the output of TextPro morphological analysis of verbs to the labels considered for tense, i.e. past, present and future, and for aspect, i.e. static, completed and in progress. *Spatial* cohesion reflects the extent to which the sentences are related by spatial particles or relations, and corresponds to the mean of location and motion ratio score. Location score is the incidence of locative prepositions (LSP) divided by LPS plus the incidence of location nouns. Location nouns are obtained from WordNet and from the Entity Recognizer of TextPro. Motion score is the incidence of motion particles (MSP) divided by MSP plus the incidence of motion verbs. Motion verbs information is extracted from WordNet as well. As for motion and locative particles, we first create a manual list, which however contains particles that can express both location and motion (for instance 'in'). The distinction between the two types of particles is based on the dependency structure of each sentence: if the particle is headed by a motion verb and dominates a location noun, then we assume that it is a motion particle. Instead, if it heads a location noun but is not dominated by a motion verb, then it is a locative particle. We are aware of the fact that this selection process is quite coarse-grained and can be biased by wrong dependency structures, ambiguity of nouns and verbs and limited extension of Italian WordNet. However, it is a viable solution to approximate the information conveyed by the corresponding indices in English, given that no clear explanation for their implementation is given.

4.3 Additional indices

We implement also three additional indices that are not part of Coh-Metrix for English. They are reported in Table 2 with the ID 41–46.

Indices 41 and 42 are based on the *Basic Italian Vocabulary* (de Mauro, 2000). This resource includes a list of 7,000 words, which were manually classified as highly familiar to native speakers of Italian. We introduce these indices because past experiments on Italian readability by Dell'Orletta et al. (2011) showed that, by combining this information with some basic features such as word and sentence length, it was possible to achieve 0.95 accuracy in a binary classification task aimed at distinguishing standard newspaper articles from simplified articles for L2 readers. Index 41 corresponds to the percentage of tokens whose base form is listed in the Basic Italian Vocabulary, while index 42 is the percentage of (unique) lemmas. The latter is the same feature implemented by Dell'Orletta et al. (2011).

Index 43 is Gulpease, computed following the formula reported in Section 4. We add it to our index list in line with Coh-Metrix, which includes also standard readability metrics such as Flesch-Reading Ease and Flesch-Kincaid.

5 The Online System

The *Coease* indices have been made available online through a Web interface at `http://readability.fbk.eu`. This allows users to copy and paste a document in the text field and to compute all available indices, similar to the functionalities of the English Coh-Metrix tool. We have normalized each index so that it is comprised between -1 and +1 using the scaling function available in LIBSVM (Chang and Lin, 2011). Low scores express low readability for the given index while high scores correspond to highly readable texts.

In order to identify the indices that are most correlated with the readability levels, we computed Pearson correlation coefficients between each index and the three classes, similar to Pitler and Nenkova

(2008). The ten most correlated indices are marked with (*) in Table 2. It is interesting to note that 6 out of 10 indices are not part of the standard Coh-Metrix framework, and account for lexical information. In all cases, correlation is moderate, being $0.3 \leq r \leq 0.6$.

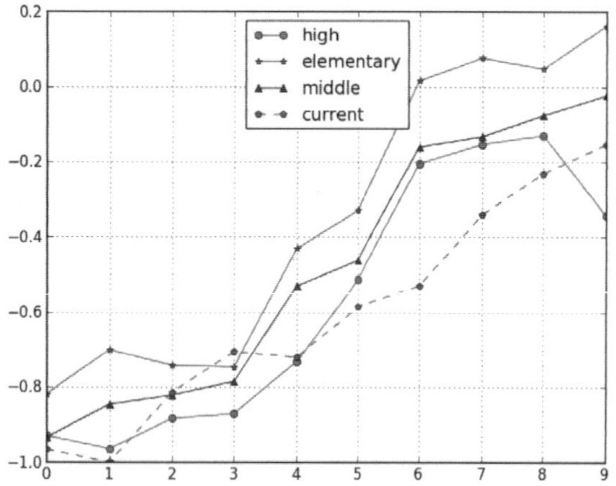

Figure 2: Graphical representation of readability as plotted by the *Coease* web interface. Index id on x axis, and normalized value on y axis

Coease is designed in order to enable users to compute readability of a given document and compare it with the average values for the three classes in our reference corpus (Section 3). Therefore, the average normalized score of each index for each class has been computed based on the corpus. Then, every time a new document is analyzed, the output scores are plotted together with the average scores for each of the three classes. This allows a user to compare different aspects of the current document, such as the lexicon or the syntax, with the averages of the three classes. For example, a user may discover that a document is highly complex from the lexical point of view, since its lexical indices are in line with those of high-school texts. However, its syntax may be rather simple, having syntax-based indices similar to those of elementary textbooks. This kind of comparison provides information that are generally not captured via supervised classification. If we trained a classifier using the indices as features, we would be able to assign a new document to elementary, middle or high-school level, but a naive user would not be able to understand how the single indices affect classification. Besides, this graphical representation allows a user to identify documents that should not be classified into a specific class, because its indices fall into different classes. Furthermore, we can detect documents with different degrees of readability within each class.

As an example, we report in Fig. 2 the graphical representation returned by the system after analyzing an article taken from 'Due Parole'[9] (labeled as 'current'), an online newspaper for adult L2 learners. The scores are compared with the average values of the 10 most correlated indices, which are reported on the x axis in the same order as they are described in Table 2. According to the plot, the article has a degree of readability similar to the 'high-school' class, although some indices show that its readability is higher (see for instance the index n. 9, i.e. lexical overlap with Class 3 documents).

The current system version returns only the 10 most correlated indices for the sake of clarity. However, it easy configurable in order to plot all indices, or just a subset selected by the user.

6 Conclusions and Future Work

We present *Coease*, a system for readability assessment of Italian inspired by Coh-Metrix principles. This set of indices improves on Gulpease index in that it takes into account discourse coherence, syntactic parsing and semantic complexity in order to account for the psycholinguistic and cognitive representations involved in reading comprehension.

We make *Coease* available through an online interface. A user can easily analyze a document and compare its readability to three difficulty levels, corresponding to average elementary, middle and high-school readability level. The graphical representation returned by the system makes this comparison straightforward, in that the indices computed for the current document are plotted together with the 10 most correlated indices in *Coease*.

In the future, we will analyze the reason why lexical indices are among the most correlated ones with the three classes. The lower impact of syntactic information, for instance, could be affected by parsing performance. However, this could depend also on how syntactic indices are computed in Coh-Metrix:

[9]http://www.dueparole.it/

we will investigate whether alternative ways to calculate the indices may be more appropriate for Italian texts.

In addition, we plan to use the indices as features for predicting the readability of unseen texts. In a classification setting, it will be interesting to see if the 10 best indices mentioned in the previous sections are also the most predictive features, given that some information may become redundant (for instance, the Gulpease index).

Acknowledgments

The work described in this paper has been partially funded by the European Commission under the contract number FP7-ICT-2009-5, Terence project.

References

Sandra Aluisio, Lucia Specia, Caroline Gasperin, and Carolina Scarton. 2010. Readability assessment for text simplification. In *Proceedings of the NAACL HLT 2010 Fifth Workshop on Innovative Use of NLP for Building Educational Applications*, pages 1–9, Stroudsburg, PA, USA.

R. H. Baayen, R. Piepenbrock, and L. Gulikers. 1995. The CELEX Lexical Database (release 2). CD-ROM.

Richard Bamberger and Erich Vanecek. 1984. *Lesen-Verstehen-Lernen-Schreiben*. Jugend un Volk Verlagsgesellschaft.

Regina Barzilay and Mirella Lapata. 2008. Modeling local coherence: An entity-based approach. *Computational Linguistics*, 34:1–34, March.

I. L. Beck, M. G. McKeown, G. M. Sinatra, and J. A. Loxterman. 1984s. Revisiting social studies text from a text-processing perspective: Evidence of improved comprehensibility. *Reading Research Quarterly*, 26:251–276.

M. G. Cataldo and J. Oakhill. 2000. Why are poor comprehenders inefficient searchers? An investigation into the effects of text representation and spatial memory on the ability to locate information in text. *Journal of Educational Psychology*, 92:791–799.

Chih-Chung Chang and Chih-Jen Lin. 2011. LIBSVM: A library for support vector machines. *ACM Transactions on Intelligent Systems and Technology*, 2:27:1–27:27. Software available at `http://www.csie.ntu.edu.tw/~cjlin/libsvm`.

Scott A. Crossley, David B. Allen, and Danielle S. McNamara. 2011. Text readability and intuitive simplification: A comparison of readability formula. *Reading in a Foreign Language*, 23(1):84–101.

Tullio de Mauro. 2000. *Il Dizionario della Lingua Italiana*. Paravia, Torino, Italy.

Felice Dell'Orletta, Simonetta Montemagni, and Giulia Venturi. 2011. READ–IT: Assessing Readability of Italian Texts with a View to Text Simplification. In *Proceedings of the Second Workshop on Speech and Language Processing for Assistive Technologies*, pages 73–83, Edinburgh, Scotland, UK, July. Association for Computational Linguistics.

T. A. Van Dijk and W. Kintsch. 1983. *Strategies of discourse comprehension*. Academic Press, New York, US.

Rudolf Flesch. 1946. *The Art of plain talk*. Harper.

V. Franchina and R. Vacca. 1986. Adaptation of Flesch readability index on a bilingual text written by the same author both in Italian and English languages. *Linguaggi*, 3:47–49.

Ingo Glöckner, Sven Hartrumpf, Hermann Helbig, Johannes Leveling, and Rainer Osswald. 2006. An architecture for rating and controlling text readability. In *Proceedings of KONVENS 2006*, pages 32–35, Konstanz, Germany, October.

A. Graesser, D. McNamara, M. Louwerse, and Z. Cai. 2004. Coh-Metrix: Analysis of text on cohesion and language. *Behavioral Research Methods, Instruments, and Computers*, 36:193–202.

Robert Gunning. 1952. *The technique of clear writing*. McGraw-Hill.

Karl F. Haberlandt and Arthur C. Graesser. 1985. Component processes in text comprehension and some of their interactions. *Journal of Experimental Psychology*, 114(3):357–374.

F. Huerta. 1959. Medida sencillas de lecturabilidad. *Consigna*, 214:29–32.

L. Kandel and A. Moles. 1958. Application de l'Indice de Flesch à la langue française. *Cahiers d'Etudes de Radio-Television*, pages 253–274.

J.P. Kincaid, R.P. Fishburne, R.L. Rogers, and B.S. Chissom. 1975. Derivation of New Readability Formulas for Navy Enlisted Personnel. *Research Branch Report*.

Alberto Lavelli and Anna Corazza. 2009. The Berkeley Parser at EVALITA 2009 Constituency Parsing Task. In *Proceedings of EVALITA Evaluation Campaign*.

A. Lavelli, J. Hall, J. Nilsson, and J. Nivre. 2009. MaltParser at the EVALITA 2009 Dependency Parsing Task. In *Proceedings of EVALITA Evaluation Campaign*.

T. Linderholm, M. G. Everson, P. van den Broek, M. Mischinski, A. Crittenden, and J. Samuels. 2000. Effects of Causal Text Revisions on More- and Less-Skilled Readers' Comprehension of Easy and Difficult Texts. *Cognition and Instruction*, 18:525–556.

Pietro Lucisano and Maria Emanuela Piemontese. 1988. Gulpease. Una formula per la predizione della difficoltà dei testi in lingua italiana. *Scuola e Città*, 3:57–68.

G. H. McLaughlin. 1969. SMOG grading: A new readability formula. *Journal of Reading*, 12(8):639–646.

D.S. McNamara, E. Kintsch, N.B. Songer, and W. Kintsch. 1996. Are good texts always better? Text coherence, background knowledge, and levels of understanding in learning from text. *Cognition and Instruction*, pages 1–43.

Emanuele Pianta, Luisa Bentivogli, and Christian Girardi. 2002. MultiWordNet: developing an aligned multilingual database. In *First International Conference on Global WordNet*, pages 292–302, Mysore, India.

Emanuele Pianta, Christian Girardi, and Roberto Zanoli. 2008. The TextPro tool suite. In *Proc. of the 6th Language Resources and Evaluation Conference (LREC)*, Marrakech, Morocco.

Emily Pitler and Ani Nenkova. 2008. Revisiting Readability: A Unified Framework for Predicting Text Quality. In *Proceedings of the 2008 Conference on Empirical Methods in Natural Language Processing*, pages 186–195, Honolulu.

Caroline E. Scarton, Daniel M. Almeida, and Sandra M. Aluísio. 2009. Análise da Inteligibilidade de textos via ferramentas de Processamento de Língua Natural: adaptando as métricas do Coh-Metrix para o Português. In *Proceedings of STIL-2009*, São Carlos, Brazil.

Tim von der Brück, Sven Hartrumpf, and Hermann Helbig. 2008. A Readability Checker with Supervised Learning using Deep Architecture. *Informatica*, 32:429–435.

Michael Wilson. 2003. *MRC Psycholinguistic Database: Machine Usable Dictionary, Version 2.00.* Rutherford Appleton Laboratory, Oxfordshire, England.

ID	Feature list
	General word and text information
	Basic Count
1-3	N. of words, sents and parag. in text
4	Mean n. of syllables per content word*
5	Mean n. of words per sentence
6	Mean n. of sentences per paragraph
	Frequencies
7	Raw frequency of content words
8	Log of raw frequency of content words
9	Min raw frequency of content words
10	Log min raw frequency of content words
	Hypernymy
11	Mean hypernym value of nouns
12	Mean hypernym value of verbs
	Syntactic indices
	Constituents information
13	Noun phrase incidence
14	Mean n. of modifiers per NP
15	Higher level constituents
16	Mean n. of words before main verb
17	Negation incidence
	Pronouns, Types, Tokens
18	Pronoun ratio
19	Type-token ratio
	Connectives
20	Incidence of all connectives
21-22	Incidence of pos./neg. additive conn.
23-24	Incidence of pos./neg. temporal conn.
25-26	Incidence of pos./neg. causal conn.
27-28	Incidence of pos./neg.* logical conn.
29	Incidence of conditional operators
	Syntactic similarity
30	Tree intersection between adj. sentences
31	Tree intersection between all sentences
	Referential and Semantic Indices
	Coreference
32	Adjacent argument overlap*
33	Stem overlap between adjacent sentences
34	Content word overlap between adj. sents.
	Situation model dimensions
35-36	Causal content and cohesion
37-38	Intentional content and cohesion*
39-40	Temporal and spatial cohesion
	Features not included in Coh-Metrix
41	Lemma overlap with VBI (token-based)*
42	Lemma overlap with VBI (type-based)*
43	Gulpease index*
44	Lexical overlap with Class 1*
45	Lexical overlap with Class 2*
46	Lexical overlap with Class 3*

Table 2: *Coease* indices for readability assessment. (*)

Do NLP and machine learning improve traditional readability formulas?

Thomas François
University of Pennsylvania
CENTAL, UCLouvain
3401 Walnut Street Suite 400A
Philadelphia, PA 19104, US
frthomas@sas.upenn.edu

Eleni Miltsakaki
University of Pennsylvania & Choosito!
3401 Walnut Street Suite 400A
Philadelphia, PA 19104, US
elenimi@seas.upenn.edu

Abstract

Readability formulas are methods used to match texts with the readers' reading level. Several methodological paradigms have previously been investigated in the field. The most popular paradigm dates several decades back and gave rise to well known readability formulas such as the Flesch formula (among several others). This paper compares this approach (henceforth "classic") with an emerging paradigm which uses sophisticated NLP-enabled features and machine learning techniques. Our experiments, carried on a corpus of texts for French as a foreign language, yield four main results: (1) the new readability formula performed better than the "classic" formula; (2) "non-classic" features were slightly more informative than "classic" features; (3) modern machine learning algorithms did not improve the explanatory power of our readability model, but allowed to better classify new observations; and (4) combining "classic" and "non-classic" features resulted in a significant gain in performance.

1 Introduction

Readability studies date back to the 1920's and have already spawned probably more than a hundred papers with research on the development of efficient methods to match readers and texts relative to their reading difficulty. During this period of time, several methodological trends have appeared in succession (reviewed in Klare (1963; 1984), DuBay (2004)). We can group these trends in three major approaches: the "classic studies", the "structuro-cognitivist paradigm" and the "AI readability", a term suggested by François (2011a).

The classic period started right after the seminal work of Vogel and Washburne (1928) and Gray and Leary (1935) and is characterized by an ideal of simplicity. The models (readability formulas) proposed to predict text difficulty for a given population are kept simple, using multiple linear regression with two, or sometimes, three predictors. The predictors are simple surface features, such as the average number of syllables per word and the average number of words per sentence. The Flesch (1948) and Dale and Chall (1948) formulas are probably the best-known examples of this period.

With the rise of cognitivism in psychological sciences in the 70's and 80's, new dimensions of texts are highlighted such as coherence, cohesion, and other discourse aspects. This led some scholars (Kintsch and Vipond, 1979; Redish and Selzer, 1985) to adopt a critical attitude to classic readability formulas which could only take into account superficial features, ignoring other important aspects contributing to text difficulty. Kintsch and Vipond (1979) and Kemper (1983), among others, suggested new features for readability, based on those newly discovered text dimensions. However, despite the fact that the proposed models made use of more sophisticated features, they failed to outperform the classic formulas. It is probably not coincidental that after these attempts readability research efforts declined in the 90s.

More recently, however, the development of efficient natural language processing (NLP) systems and the success of machine learning methods led to a resurgence of interest in readability as it became clear that these developments could impact the design and performance of readability measures. Several studies (Si and Callan, 2001; Collins-Thompson and Callan, 2005; Schwarm and Ostendorf, 2005; Feng et al., 2010) have used NLP-enabled feature extraction and state-of-the-art machine learning algorithms and have reported significant gains in performance, suggesting that the AI approach might be superior to previous attempts.

Going beyond reports of performance which are often hard to compare due to a lack of a common gold standard, we are interested in investigating AI approaches more closely with the aim of understanding the reasons behind the reported superiority over classic formulas. AI readability systems use NLP for richer feature extraction and a machine learning algorithm. Given that the classic formulas are also statistical, is performance boosted because of the addition of NLP-enabled feature extraction or by better machine learning algorithms? In this paper, we report initial findings of three experiments designed to explore this question.

The paper is organized as follows. Section 2 reviews previous findings in the field and the challenge of providing a uniform explanation for these findings. Section 3 gives a brief overview of prior work on French readability, which is the context of our experiments (evaluating the readability of French texts). Because there is no prior work comparing classic formulas with AI readablity measures for French, we first report the results of this comparison in Section 3. Then, we proceed with the results of three experiments (2-4), comparing the contributions of the AI enabled features with features used in classic formulas, different machine learning algorithms and the interactions of features with algorithms. There results are reported in Sections 4, 5, and 6, respectively. We conclude in Section 7 with a summary of the main findings and future work.

2 Previous findings

Several readability studies in the past decade have reported a performance gain when using NLP-enabled features, language models, and machine learning algorithms to evaluate the reading difficulty of a variety of texts (Si and Callan, 2001; Collins-Thompson and Callan, 2005; Schwarm and Ostendorf, 2005; Heilman et al., 2008; Feng et al., 2010).

A first explanation for this superiority would be related to the new predictors used in recent models. Classic formulas relied mostly on surface lexical and syntactic variables such as the average number of words per sentence, the average number of letters per word, the proportion of given POS tags in the text or the proportion of out-of-simple-vocabulary words. In the AI paradigm, several new features have been added, including language models, parse tree-based predictors, probability of discourse relations, estimates of text coherence, etc. It is reasonable to assume that these new features capture a wider range of readability factors thus bringing into the models more and, possibly, better information.

However, the evidence from comparative studies is not consistent on this question. In several cases, AI models include features central to classic formulas which, when isolated, appear to be the stronger predictors in the models. An exception to this trend is the work of Pitler and Nenkova (2008) who reported non-significant correlation for the mean number of words per sentence ($r = 0.1637, p = 0.3874$) and the mean number of characters per word ($r = -0.0859, p = 0.6519$). In their study, though, they used text quality rather than text difficulty as the dependent variable. The data consisted solely of text from the Wall Street Journal which is "intended for an educated adult audience" text labelled for degrees of reading fluency. Feng et al. (2010) compared a set of similar variables and observed that language models performed better than classic formula features but classic formula features outperformed those based on parsing information. Collins-Thompson and Callan (2005) found that the classic type-token ratio or number of words not in the 3000-words Dale list appeared to perform better than their language model on a corpus from readers, but were poorer predictors on web-extracted texts.

In languages other than English, François (2011b) surveyed a wide range of features for French and reports that the feature that uses a limited vocabulary list (just like in some classic formulas) has a stronger correlation with reading difficulty that a unigram model and the best performing syntactic feature was the average number of words per sentences. Aluisio et al. (2010), also, found that the best correlate with difficulty was the average number of words per sentence. All in all, while there is sufficient evidence that the AI paradigm outperforms the classis formulas, classic features have often been shown to make the single strongest predictors.

An alternative explanation could be that, by comparison to the simpler statistical analyses that determined the coefficients of the classic formulas, machine learning algorithms, such as support machine vector (SVM) or logistic regression are more sophisticated and better able to learn the regularities in training data, thus building more accurate models. Work in this direction has been of smaller scale but already reporting inconsistent results. Heilman et al. (2008) considered the performance of linear regression, ordinal and multinomial logistic regression, and found the latter to be more efficient. However, Kate et al. (2010) obtained contradictory findings, showing that regression-based algorithms perform better, especially when regression trees are used for bagging. For French, François (2011b) found that SVMs were more efficient than linear regression, ordinal and multinomial logistic regression, boosting, and bagging.

Finally, it is quite possible that there are interactions between types of features and types of statistical algorithms and these interactions are primarily responsible for the better performance.

In what follows, we present the results of three studies (experiments 2-4), comparing the contributions of the AI enabled features with features used in classic formulas, different machine learning algorithms and the interactions of features with algorithms. As mentioned earlier, all the studies have been done on French data, consisting of text extracted from levelled FFL textbooks (French as Foreign Language). Because there is no prior work comparing classic formulas with AI readability measures for FFL, we first report the results of this comparison in the next section (experiment 1).

3 Experiment 1: Model comparison for FFL

To compute a classic readability formula for FFL, we used the formula proposed for French by Kandel and Moles (1958). We compared the results of this formula with the AI model trained on the FFL data used by François (2011b).

The Kandel and Moles (1958) formula is an adaptation of the Flesch formula for French, based on a study of a bilingual corpus:

$$Y = 207 - 1.015lp - 0.736lm \quad (1)$$

where Y is a readability score ranging from 100 (easiest) to 0 (harder); lp is the average number of words per sentence and lm is the average number of syllables per 100 words. Although this formula is not specifically designed for FFL, we chose to implement it over formulas proposed for FFL (Tharp, 1939; Uitdenbogerd, 2005). FFL-specific formulas are optimized for English-speaking learners of French while our dataset is agnostic to the native language of the learners.

The computation of the Kandel and Moles (1958) formula requires a syllabification system for French. Due to unavailability of such a system for French, we adopted a hybrid syllabification method. For words included in Lexique (New et al., 2004), we used the gold syllabification included in the dictionary. For all other words, we generated API phonetic representations with espeak [1], and then applied the syllabification tool used for Lexique3 (Pallier, 1999). The accuracy of this process exceeded 98%.

For the comparison with an AI model, we extracted the same 46 features (see Table 2 for the complete list) used in François' model [2] and trained a SVM model.

For all the study, the gold-standard consisted of data taken from textbooks and labeled according to the classification made by the publishers. The corpus includes a wide range of texts, including extracts from novels, newspapers articles, songs, mail, dialogue, etc. The difficulty levels are defined by the Common European Framework of Reference for Languages (CEFR) (Council of Europe, 2001) as follows: A1 (Breakthrough); A2 (Waystage); B1 (Threshold); B2 (Vantage); C1 (Effective Operational Proficiency) and C2 (Mastery). The test corpus includes 68 texts per level, for a total of 408 documents (see Table 1).

We applied both readability models to this test corpus. Assessing and comparing the performance

[1] Available at: http://espeak.sourceforge.net/.

[2] Details on how to implement these features can be found in François (2011b).

A1	A2	B1	B2	C1	C2	Total
$68(10,827)$	$68(12,045)$	$68(17,781)$	$68(25,546)$	$68(92,327)$	$68(39,044)$	$408(127,681)$

Table 1: Distribution of the number of texts and tokens per level in our test corpus.

of the two models with accuracy scores (acc), as is common in classification tasks, has proved challenging and, in the end, uninformative. This is because the Kandel and Moles formula's output scores are not an ordinal variable, but intervals. To compute accuracy we would have to define a set of rather arbitrary cut off points in the intervals and correspond them with level boundaries. We tried three approaches to achieve this task. First, we used correspondences between Flesch scores and seven difficulty levels proposed for French by de Landsheere (1963): "very easy" (70 to 80) to "very difficult" (-20 to 10). Collapsing the "difficult" and "very difficult" categories into one, we were able to roughly match this scale with the A1-C2 scale. The second method was similar, except that those levels were mapped on the values from the original Flesch scale instead of the one adapted for French. The third approach was to estimate normal distribution parameters μ_j and σ_j for each level j for the Kandel and Moles' formula output scores obtained on our corpus. The class membership of a given observation i was then computed as follows:

$$\arg\max_{j=1}^{6} P(i \in j \mid N(\mu_j, \sigma_j)) \qquad (2)$$

Since the parameters were trained on the same corpus used for the evaluation, this computation should yield optimal class membership thresholds for our data.

Given the limitations of all three approaches, it is not surprising that accuracy scores were very low: 9% for the first and 12% for the second, which is worse than random (16.6%). The third approach gave a much improved accuracy score, 33%, but still quite low. The problem is that, in a continuous formula, predictions that are very close to the actual will be classified as errors if they fall on the wrong side of the cut off threshold. These results are, in any case, clearly inferior to the AI formula based on SVM, which classified correctly 49% of the texts.

A more suitable evaluation measure for a continuous formula would be to compute the multiple correlation (R). The multiple correlation indicates the extent to which predictions are close to the actual classes, and, when R^2 is used, it describes the percentage of the dependent variable variation which is explained by the model. Kandel and Moles' formula got a slightly better performance ($R = 0.551$), which is still substantially lower that the score ($R = 0.728$) obtained for the SVM model. To check if the difference between the two correlation scores was significant, we applied the Hotelling's T-test for dependent correlation (Hotelling, 1940) (required given that the two models were evaluated on the same data). The result of the test is highly significant ($t = -19.5; p = 1.83^{e-60}$), confirming that the SVM model performed better that the classic formula.

Finally, we computed a partial Spearman correlation for both models. We considered the output of each model as a single variable and we could, therefore, evaluate the relative predictive power of each variable when the other variable is controlled. The partial correlation for the Kandel and Moles formula is very low ($\rho = -0.11$; $p = 0.04$) while the SVM model retains a good partial correlation ($\rho = -0.53; p < 0.001$).

4 Experiment 2: Comparison of features

In this section, we compared the contribution of the features used in classic formulas with the more sophisticated NLP-enabled features used in the machine learning models of readability. Given that the features used in classic formulas are very easy to compute and require minimal processing by comparison to the NLP features that require heavy preprocessing (e.g., parsing), we are, also, interested in finding out how much gain we obtain from the NLP features. A consideration that becomes important for tasks requiring real time evaluation of reading difficulty.

To evaluate the relative contribution of each set of features, we experiment with two sets of features (see Table 2. We labeled as "classic", not only

Family	Tag	Description of the variable	ρ	Linear
Classic	PA-Alterego	Proportion of absent words from a list of easy words from *AlterEgo1*	0.652	No
	X90FFFC	90th percentile of inflected forms for content words only	-0.641	No
	X75FFFC	75th percentile of inflected forms for content words only	-0.63	No
	PA-Goug2000	Proportion of absent words from 2000 first of Gougenheim et al. (1964)'s list	0.597	No
	MedianFFFC	Median of the frequencies of inflected content words	-0.56	Yes
	PM8	Pourcentage of words longer than 8 characters	0.525	No
	NL90P	Length of the word corresponding to the 90th percentile of word lengths	0.521	No
	NLM	Mean number of letters per word	0.483	Yes
	IQFFFC	Interquartile range of the frequencies of inflected content words	0.405	No
	MeanFFFC	Mean of the frequencies of inflected content words	-0.319	No
	TTR	Type-token ratio based on lemma	0.284	No
	NMP	Mean number of words per sentence	0.618	No
	NWS90	Length (in words) of the 90th percentile sentence	0.61	No
	PL30	Percentage of sentences longer than 30 words	0.56	Yes
	PRE/PRO	Ratio of prepositions and pronouns	0.345	Yes
	GRAM/PRO	Ratio of grammatical words and pronouns	0.34	Yes
	ART/PRO	Ratio of articles and pronouns	0.326	Yes
	PRE/ALL	Proportions of prepositions in the text	0.326	Yes
	PRE/LEX	Ratio of prepositions and lexical words	0.322	Yes
	ART/LEX	Ratio of articles and lexical words	0.31	Yes
	PRE/GRAM	Ratio of prepositions and grammatical words	0.304	Yes
	NOM-NAM/ART	Ratio of nouns (common and proper) and gramm. words	-0.29	Yes
	PP1P2	Percentage of P1 and P2 personal pronouns	-0.333	No
	PP2	Percentage of P2 personal pronouns	-0.325	Yes
	PPD	Percentage of personal pronouns of dialogue	0.318	No
	BINGUI	Presence of commas	$0,462$	No
Non-classic	Unigram	Probability of the text sequence based on unigrams	0.546	No
	MeanNGProb-G	Average probability of the text bigrams based on Google	0.407	Yes
	FCNeigh75	75th percentile of the cumulated frequency of neighbors per word	-0.306	Yes
	MedNeigh+Freq	Median number of more frequent neighbor for words	-0.229	Yes
	Neigh+Freq90	90th percentile of more frequent neighbor for words	-0.192	Yes
	PPres	Presence of at least one present participle in the text	0.44	No
	PPres-C	Proportion of present participle among verbs	0.41	Yes
	PPasse	Presence of at least one past participle	0.388	No
	Infi	Presence of at least one infinive	0.341	No
	Impf	Presence of at least one imperfect	0.272	No
	Subp	Presence of at least one subjunctive present	0.266	Yes
	Futur	Presence of at least one future	0.252	No
	Cond	Presence of at least one conditional	0.227	No
	PasseSim	Presence of at least one simple past	0.146	No
	Imperatif	Presence of at least one imperative	0.019	Yes
	Subi	Presence of at least one subjunctive imperfect	0.049	Yes
	avLocalLsa-Lem	Average intersentential cohesion measured via LSA	$0,63$	No
	ConcDens	Estimate of the conceptual density with *Densidées* (Lee et al., 2010)	0.253	Yes
	NAColl	Proportion of MWE having the structure NOUN ADJ	0.286	Yes
	NCPW	Average number of MWEs per word	0.135	Yes

Table 2: List of the 46 features used by François (2011b) in his model. The Spearman correlation reported here also comes from this study.

the features that are commonly used in traditional formulas like Flesch (length of words and number of words per sentence) but also other easy to compute features that were identified in readability work. Specifically, in the "classic" set we include number of personal pronouns (given as a list) (Gray and Leary, 1935), the Type Token Ratio (TTR) (Lively and Pressey, 1923), or even simple ratios of POS (Bormuth, 1966).

The "non-classic" set includes more complex NLP-enabled features (coherence measured through LSA, MWE, n-grams, etc.) and features suggested by the structuro-cognitivist research (e.g., information about tense and variables based on orthographical neighbors).

For evaluation, we first computed and compared the average bivariate correlations of both sets. This test yielded a better correlation for the classic features ($\bar{r} = 0.48$ over the non-classic features $\bar{r} = 0.29$)

As a second test, we trained a SVM model on each set and evaluated performances in a ten-fold cross-validation. For this test, we reduced the number of classic features by six to equal the number of predictors of the non-classic set. Our hypothesis was the SVM model using non-classic features would outperform the classic set because the non-classic features bring richer information. This assumption was not strictly confirmed as the non-classic set performed only slightly better than the classic set. The difference in the correlation scores was small (0.01) and non-significant ($t(9) = 0.49; p = 0.32$), but the difference in accuracy was larger (3.8%) and close to significance ($t(9) = 1.50; p = 0.08$). Then, in an effort to pin down the source of the SVM gain that did not come out in the comparison above, we defined a SVM baseline model (b) that included only two typical features of the classic set: the average number of letter per word (NLM) and the average number of word per sentence (NMP). Then, for each of the i remaining variables (44), we trained a model m_i including three predictors: NLM, NMP, and i. The difference between the correlation of the baseline model and that of the model m_i was interpreted as the information gain carried by the feature i. Therefore, for both sets, of cardinality N_s, we computed:

$$\frac{\sum_{i=1}^{N_s} R(m_i) - R(b)}{N_s} \tag{3}$$

where $R(m_i)$ is the multiple correlation of model m_i.

Our assumption was that, if the non-classic set brings in more varied information, every predictor should, on average, improve more the R of the baseline model, while the classic variables, more redundant with NLM and NP, would be less efficient. In this test, the mean gain for R was 0.017 for the classic set and 0.022 for the non-classic set. Although the difference was once more small, this test yielded a similar trend than the previous test.

As a final test, we compared the performance of the SVM model trained only on the "classic" set with the SVM trained on both sets. In this case, the improvement was significant ($t(9) = 3.82; p = 0.002$) with accuracy rising from 37.5% to 49%. Although this test does not help us decide on the nature of the gain as it could be coming just from the increased number of features, it shows that combining "classic" and "non-classic" variables is valuable.

5 Experiment 3: Comparison of statistical models

In this section, we explore the hypothesis that AI models outperform classic formulas because they use better statistical algorithms. We compare the performance of a"classic" algorithm, multiple linear regression, with the performance of a machine learning algorithm, in this case SVM. Note that an SVMs have an advantage over linear regression for features non-linearly related with difficulty. Bormuth (1966, 98-102) showed that several classic features, especially those focusing on the word level, were indeed non-linear. To control for linearity, we split the 46 features into a linear and a non-linear subset, using the Guilford's F test for linearity (Guilford, 1965) and an $\alpha = 0.05$. This classification yielded two equal sets of 23 variables (see Table 2). In Table 3, we report the performance of the four models in terms of R, accuracy, and adjacent accuracy. Following, Heilman et al. (2008), we define "adjacent accuracy" as the proportion of predictions that were within one level of the assigned label in the corpus.

	Model	R	Acc.	Adj. acc.
Linear	LR	0.58	27%	72%
	SVM	0.64	38%	73%
Non-Linear	LR	0.75	36%	81%
	SVM	0.70	44%	76%

Table 3: Multiple correlation coefficient (R), accuracy and adjacent accuracy for linear regression and SVM models, using the set of features either linearly or non linearly related to difficulty.

Adjacent accuracy is closer to R as it is less sensitive to minor classification errors.

Our results showed a contradictory pattern, yielding a different result depending on type of evaluation: accuracy or R and adjacent accuracy. With respect to accuracy scores, the SVM performed better in the classification task, with a significant performance gain for both linear (gain = 9%; $t(9) = 2.42; p = 0.02$) and non-linear features (gain = 8%; $t(9) = 3.01; p = 0.007$). On the other hand, the difference in R was non-significant for linear (gain = 0.06; $t(9) = 0.80; p = 0.22$) and even negative and close to significance for non-linear (gain = -0.05; $t(9) = 1.61; p = 0.07$). In the light of these results, linear regression (LR) appears to be as efficient as SVM accounting for variation in the dependant variable (their R^2 are pretty similar), but produces poorer predictions.

This is an interesting finding, which suggests that the contradictory results in prior literature with regard to performance of different readability models (see Section 2) might be related to the evaluation measure used. Heilman et al. (2008, 7), who compared linear and logistic regressions, found that the R of the linear model was significantly higher than the R of the logistic model ($p < 0.01$). In contrast, the logistic model behaved significantly better ($p < 0.01$) in terms of adjacent accuracy. Similarly, Kate and al. (2010, 548), which used R as evaluation measure, reported that their preliminary results "verified that regression performed better than classification". Once they compared linear regression and SVM regression, they noticed similar correlations for both techniques (respectively 0.7984 and 0.7915).

To conclude this section, our findings suggest that (1) linear regression and SVM are comparable in accounting for the variance of text difficulty and (2) SVM has significantly better accuracy scores than linear regression.

6 Experiment 4: Combined evaluation

In Experiment 2, we saw that "non-classic" features are slightly, but non-significantly, better than the "classic" features. In Experiment 3, we saw that SVM performs better than linear regression when the evaluation is done by accuracy but both demonstrate similar explanatory power in accounting for the variation. In this section, we report evaluation results for four models, derived by combining two sets of features, classic and non-classic, with two algorithms, linear regression and SVM. The results are shown in Table (4).

The results are consistent with the findings in the previous sections. When evaluated with accuracy scores SVM performs better with both classic ($t(9) = 3.15; p = 0.006$) and non-classic features ($t(9) = 3.32; p = 0.004$). The larger effect obtained for the non-classic features might be due to an interaction, i.e., an SVM trained with non-classic features might be better at discriminating reading levels. However, with respect to R, both algorithms are similar, with linear regression outperforming SVM in adjacent accuracy (non-significant). Linear regression and SVM, then, appear to have equal explanatory power.

As regards the type of features, the explanatory power of both models seems to increase with non-classic features as shown in the increased R, although significance is not reached ($t(9) = 0.49; p = 0.32$ for the regression and $t(9) = 1.5; p = 0.08$ for the SVM).

7 General discussion and conclusions

Recent readability studies have provided preliminary evidence that the evaluation of readability using NLP-enabled features and sophisticated machine learning algorithms outperform the classic readability formulas, such as Flesch, which rely on surface textual features. In this paper, we reported a number of experiments the purpose of which was to identify the source of this performance gain.

Specifically, we compared the performance of classic and non-classic features and the performance

	Model	R	Acc.	Adj. acc.
Classic	LR	0.66	30.6%	78%
	SVM	0.67	37.5%	76%
Non-classic	LR	0.68	32%	76%
	SVM	0.68	41.8%	73%

Table 4: Multiple correlation coefficient (R), accuracy and adjacent accuracy for linear regression and SVM models with either the classic or the non-classic set of predictors.

of two statistical algorithms: linear regression (used in classic formulas) and SVM (in the context of FFL readability). Our results indicate that classic features are strong single predictors of readability. While we were not able to show that the non-classic features are better predictors by themselves, our findings show that leaving out non-classic features has a significant negative impact on the performance. The best performance was obtained when both classic and non-classic features were used.

Our experiments on the comparison of the two statistical algorithms showed that the SVM outperforms linear regression by a measure of accuracy, but the two algorithms are comparable in explanatory power accounting for the same amount of variability. This observation accounts for contradictory conclusions reported in previous work. Our study shows that different evaluation measures can lead to quite different conclusions.

Finally, our comparison of four models derived by combining linear regression and SVM with "classic" and "non-classic" features confirms the significant contribution of "non-classic" features and the SVM algorithm to classification accuracy. However, by a measure of *adjacent accuracy* and explanatory power, the two algorithms are comparable.

From a practical application point of view, it would be interesting to try these algorithms in web applications that process large amounts of text in real time (e.g., READ-X (Miltsakaki, 2009)) to evaluate the trade-offs between accuracy and efficiency.

Acknowledgments

We would like to acknowledge the invaluable help of Bernadette Dehottay for the collection of the corpus, as well as the Belgian American Educational Foundation that supported Dr. Thomas François with a Fellowship during this work.

References

S. Aluisio, L. Specia, C. Gasperin, and C. Scarton. 2010. Readability assessment for text simplification. In *Fifth Workshop on Innovative Use of NLP for Building Educational Applications*, pages 1–9, Los Angeles.

J.R. Bormuth. 1966. Readability: A new approach. *Reading research quarterly*, 1(3):79–132.

K. Collins-Thompson and J. Callan. 2005. Predicting reading difficulty with statistical language models. *Journal of the American Society for Information Science and Technology*, 56(13):1448–1462.

Council of Europe. 2001. *Common European Framework of Reference for Languages: Learning, Teaching, Assessment.* Press Syndicate of the University of Cambridge.

E. Dale and J.S. Chall. 1948. A formula for predicting readability. *Educational research bulletin*, 27(1):11–28.

G. de Landsheere. 1963. Pour une application des tests de lisibilité de Flesch à la langue française. *Le Travail Humain*, 26:141–154.

W.H. DuBay. 2004. *The principles of readability.* Impact Information. Disponible sur http://www.nald.ca/library/research/readab/readab.pdf.

L. Feng, M. Jansche, M. Huenerfauth, and N. Elhadad. 2010. A Comparison of Features for Automatic Readability Assessment. In *COLING 2010: Poster Volume*, pages 276–284.

R. Flesch. 1948. A new readability yardstick. *Journal of Applied Psychology*, 32(3):221–233.

T. François. 2011a. La lisibilité computationnelle : un renouveau pour la lisibilité du français langue première et seconde ? *International Journal of Applied Linguistics (ITL)*, 160:75–99.

T. François. 2011b. *Les apports du traitement automatique du langage à la lisibilité du franais langue étrangère*. Ph.D. thesis, Université Catholique de Louvain. Thesis Supervisors : Cédrick Fairon and Anne Catherine Simon.

G. Gougenheim, R. Michéa, P. Rivenc, and A. Sauvageot. 1964. *Lélaboration du français fondamental (1er degré).* Didier, Paris.

W.S. Gray and B.E. Leary. 1935. *What makes a book readable*. University of Chicago Press, Chicago: Illinois.

J.P. Guilford. 1965. *Fundamental statistics in psychology and education*. McGraw-Hill, New-York.

M. Heilman, K. Collins-Thompson, and M. Eskenazi. 2008. An analysis of statistical models and features for reading difficulty prediction. In *Proceedings of the Third Workshop on Innovative Use of NLP for Building Educational Applications*, pages 1–8.

H. Hotelling. 1940. The selection of variates for use in prediction with some comments on the general problem of nuisance parameters. *The Annals of Mathematical Statistics*, 11(3):271–283.

L. Kandel and A. Moles. 1958. Application de l'indice de Flesch à la langue française. *Cahiers Études de Radio-Télévision*, 19:253–274.

R. Kate, X. Luo, S. Patwardhan, M. Franz, R. Florian, R. Mooney, S. Roukos, and C. Welty. 2010. Learning to predict readability using diverse linguistic features. In *Proceedings of the 23rd International Conference on Computational Linguistics (Coling 2010)*, pages 546–554.

S. Kemper. 1983. Measuring the inference load of a text. *Journal of Educational Psychology*, 75(3):391–401.

W. Kintsch and D. Vipond. 1979. Reading comprehension and readability in educational practice and psychological theory. In L.G. Nilsson, editor, *Perspectives on Memory Research*, pages 329–365. Lawrence Erlbaum, Hillsdale, NJ.

G.R.. Klare. 1963. *The Measurement of Readability*. Iowa State University Press, Ames, IA.

G.R. Klare. 1984. Readability. In P.D. Pearson, R. Barr, M. L. Kamil, P. Mosenthal, and R. Dykstra, editors, *Handbook of Reading Research*, pages 681–744. Longman, New York.

H. Lee, P. Gambette, E. Maillé, and C. Thuillier. 2010. Densidées: calcul automatique de la densité des idées dans un corpus oral. In *Actes de la douxime Rencontre des tudiants Chercheurs en Informatique pour le Traitement Automatique des langues (RECITAL)*.

B.A. Lively and S.L. Pressey. 1923. A method for measuring the vocabulary burden of textbooks. *Educational Administration and Supervision*, 9:389–398.

E. Miltsakaki. 2009. Matching readers' preferences and reading skills with appropriate web texts. In *Proceedings of the 12th Conference of the European Chapter of the Association for Computational Linguistics: Demonstrations Session*, pages 49–52.

B. New, C. Pallier, M. Brysbaert, and L. Ferrand. 2004. Lexique 2: A new French lexical database. *Behavior Research Methods, Instruments, & Computers*, 36(3):516.

C. Pallier. 1999. Syllabation des représentations phonétiques de brulex et de lexique. Technical report, Technical Report, update 2004. Lien: http://www. pallier. org/ressources/syllabif/syllabation. pdf.

E. Pitler and A. Nenkova. 2008. Revisiting readability: A unified framework for predicting text quality. In *Proceedings of the Conference on Empirical Methods in Natural Language Processing*, pages 186–195.

J.C. Redish and J. Selzer. 1985. The place of readability formulas in technical communication. *Technical communication*, 32(4):46–52.

S.E. Schwarm and M. Ostendorf. 2005. Reading level assessment using support vector machines and statistical language models. *Proceedings of the 43rd Annual Meeting on Association for Computational Linguistics*, pages 523–530.

L. Si and J. Callan. 2001. A statistical model for scientific readability. In *Proceedings of the Tenth International Conference on Information and Knowledge Management*, pages 574–576. ACM New York, NY, USA.

J.B. Tharp. 1939. The Measurement of Vocabulary Difficulty. *Modern Language Journal*, pages 169–178.

S. Uitdenbogerd. 2005. Readability of French as a foreign language and its uses. In *Proceedings of the Australian Document Computing Symposium*, pages 19–25.

M. Vogel and C. Washburne. 1928. An objective method of determining grade placement of children's reading material. *The Elementary School Journal*, 28(5):373–381.

Comparing human versus automatic feature extraction for fine-grained elementary readability assessment

Yi Ma, Ritu Singh, Eric Fosler-Lussier
Dept. of Computer Science & Engineering
The Ohio State University
Columbus, OH 43210, USA
may,singhri,fosler@cse.ohio-state.edu

Robert Lofthus
Xerox Corporation
Rochester, NY 14604, USA
Robert.Lofthus@xerox.com

Abstract

Early primary children's literature poses some interesting challenges for automated readability assessment: for example, teachers often use fine-grained reading leveling systems for determining appropriate books for children to read (many current systems approach readability assessment at a coarser whole grade level). In previous work (Ma et al., 2012), we suggested that the fine-grained assessment task can be approached using a ranking methodology, and incorporating features that correspond to the visual layout of the page improves performance. However, the previous methodology for using "found" text (e.g., scanning in a book from the library) requires human annotation of the text regions and correction of the OCR text. In this work, we ask whether the annotation process can be automated, and also experiment with richer syntactic features found in the literature that can be automatically derived from either the human-corrected or raw OCR text. We find that automated visual and text feature extraction work reasonably well and can allow for scaling to larger datasets, but that in our particular experiments the use of syntactic features adds little to the performance of the system, contrary to previous findings.

1 Introduction

Knowing the reading level of a children's book is an important task in the educational setting. Teachers want to have leveling for books in the school library; parents are trying to select appropriate books for their children; writers need guidance while writing for different literacy needs (e.g. text simplification)—reading level assessment is required in a variety of contexts. The history of assessing readability using simple arithmetic metrics dates back to the 1920s when Thorndike (1921) has measured difficulty of texts by tabulating words according to the frequency of their use in general literature. Most of the traditional readability formulas were also based on countable features of text, such as syllable counts (Flesch, 1948).

More advanced machine learning techniques such as classification and regression have been applied to the task of reading level prediction (Collins-Thompson and Callan, 2004; Schwarm and Ostendorf, 2005; Petersen and Ostendorf, 2009; Feng et al., 2010); such works are described in further detail in the next Section 2. In recent work (Ma et al., 2012), we approached the problem of fine-grained leveling of books, demonstrating that a ranking approach to predicting reading level outperforms both classification and regression approaches in that domain. A further finding was that visually-oriented features that consider the visual layout of the page (e.g. number of text lines per annotated text region, text region area compared to the whole page area and font size etc.) play an important role in predicting the reading levels of children's books in which pictures and textual layout dominate the book content over text.

However, the data preparation process in our previous study involves human intervention—we ask human annotators to draw rectangle markups around text region over pages. Moreover, we only use a very shallow surface level text-based feature set to compare with the visually-oriented features. Hence in this paper, we assess the effect of using completely automated annotation processing within the same framework. We are interested in exploring how much performance will change by completely eliminating manual intervention. At the same time, we have also extended our previous feature set by introducing a richer set of automatically derived text-based features, proposed by Feng *et al.* (2010), which capture deeper syntactic complexities of the text. Unlike our previous work, the major goal of this paper is not trying to compare different machine learning techniques used in readability assessment task, but rather to compare the performance differences between with and without human labor involved within our previous proposed system framework.

We begin the paper with the description of related work in Section 2, followed by detailed explanation regarding data preparation and automatic annotations in Section 3. The extended features will be covered in Section 4, followed by experimental analysis in Section 5, in which we will compare the results between human annotations and automatic annotations. We will also report the system performance after incorporating the rich text features (structural features). Conclusions follow in Section 6.

2 Related Work

Since 1920, approximately 200 readability formulas have been reported in the literature (DuBay, 2004); statistical language processing techniques have recently entered into the fray for readability assessment. Si and Callan (2001) and Collins-Thompson and Callan (2004) have demonstrated the use of language models is more robust for web documents and passages. Heilman *et al.* (2007) studied the impact of grammar-based features combined with language modeling approach for readability assessment of first and second language texts. They argued that grammar-based features are more pertinent for second language learners than for the first language readers. Schwarm and Ostendorf (2005) and Petersen and Ostendorf (2009) both used a support vector machine to classify texts based on the reading level. They combined traditional methods of readability assessment and the features from language models and parsers. Aluisio *et al.* (2010) have developed a tool for text simplification for the authoring process which addresses lexical and syntactic phenomena to make text readable but their assessment takes place at more coarse levels of literacy instead of finer-grained levels used for children's books.

A detailed analysis of various features for automatic readability assessment has been done by Feng *et al.* (2010). Most of the previous work has used web page documents, short passages or articles from educational newspapers as their datasets; typically the task is to assess reading level at a whole-grade level. In contrast, early primary children's literature is typically leveled in a more fine-grained manner, and the research question we pursued in our previous study was to investigate appropriate methods of predicting what we suspected was a non-linear reading level scale.

Automating the process of readability assessment is crucial for eventual widespread acceptance. Previous studies have looked at documents that were already found in electronic form, such as web texts. While e-books are certainly on the rise (and would help automated processing) it is unlikely that paper books will be completely eliminated from the primary school classroom soon. Our previous study required both manual scanning of the books and manual annotation of the books to extract the location and content of text within the book — the necessity of which we evaluate in this study by examining the effects of errors from the digitization process.

3 Data Preparation and Book Annotation

Our previous study was based on a corpus of 36 scanned children's books; in this study we have expanded the set to 97 books which range from levels A to N in Fountas and Pinnell Benchmark Assessment System 1 (Fountas and Pinnell, 2010); the Fountas and Pinnell level serves as our gold standard. The distribution of number of books per reading level is shown in Table 1. Levels A to N, in increasing difficulty, corresponds to the primary grade books from roughly kindergarten through third grade. The collection of children's books covers a large diversity of genres, series and publishers.

Reading Level	# of Books	Reading Level	# of Books
A	6	H	7
B	9	I	6
C	5	J	11
D	8	K	6
E	11	L	3
F	10	M	6
G	7	N	2

Table 1: Distribution of books over Fountas and Pinnell reading levels

Our agreement with the books' publishers only allows access to physical copies of books rather than electronic versions; we scan each book into a PDF version. This situation would be similar to that of a contemporary classroom teacher who is selecting books from the classroom or school library for evaluating a child's literacy progress.[1] We then use Adobe Acrobat to run OCR (Optical Character Recognition) on the PDF books. Following our previous work, we first begin our process of annotating each book using Adobe Acrobat before converting them into corresponding XML files. Features for each book are extracted from their corresponding XMLs which contain all the text information and book layout contents necessary to calculate the features. Each book is manually scanned, and then annotated in two different ways: we use human annotators (Section 3.1) and a completely automated process (Section 3.2). The job of human annotators is primarily to eliminate the errors made by OCR software, as well as correctly identifying text regions on each page. We encountered three types of typical OCR errors for the children's books in our set:

1. False alarms: some small illustration picture segments (e.g. flower patterns on a little girl's pajama or grass growing in bunches on the ground) are recognized as text.

2. False negatives: this is more likely to occur for text on irregular background such as white text on black background or text overlapped with illustrations.

3. OCR could misread the text. These are most common errors. Some examples of this type of error are shown in Table 2.

[1]While it is clear that publishers will be moving toward electronic books which would avoid the process of scanning (and likely corresponding OCR problems), it is also clear that physical books and documents will be present in the classroom for years to come.

OCR output	Correct word	Example
1	I	1 – I
!	I	! – I
[	f	[or – for
O	0	1OO – 100
nn	rm	wann – warm
rn	m	horne – home
IT!	m	aIT! – am
1n	m	tilne – time
n1.	m	n1.y – my
1V	W	1Ve – We
vv	w	vvhen – when

Table 2: Some common OCR errors

The two different annotation processes are explained in the following Subsections 3.1 and 3.2.

3.1 Human Annotation

Annotators manually draw a rectangular box over the text region on each page using Adobe Acrobat markup drawing tools. The annotators also correct the type 2 and 3 of OCR errors which are mentioned above. In human annotation process, the false alarm (type 1) errors are implicitly prevented since the annotators will only annotate the regions where text truly exists on the page (no matter whether the OCR recognized or not).

3.2 Automatic Annotation

For automatic annotation, we make use of JavaScript API provided by Adobe Acrobat. The automatic annotation tool is implemented as a JavaScript plugin menu item within Adobe Acrobat. The JavaScript API can return the position of every single recognized word on the page. Based on the position cues of each word, we design a simple algorithm to automatically cluster the words into separate groups according to certain spatial distance thresholds.[2] In-

[2]A distance threshold of 22 pixels was used in practice.

tuitively, one could imagine the words as small floating soap bubbles on the page—where smaller bubbles (individual words) which are close enough will merge together to form bigger bubbles (text regions) automatically. For each detected text region, a bounding rectangle box annotation is drawn on the page automatically. Beyond this point, the rest of the data preparation process is identical to human annotation, in which the corresponding XMLs will be generated from the annotated versions of the PDF books. However, unlike human annotation, automating the annotation process can introduce noise into the data due to uncorrected OCR errors. In correspondence to the three types of OCR errors, automatic annotation could also draw extra bounding rectangle boxes on non-text region (where OCR thinks there is text there but there is not), fails to draw bounding rectangle boxes on text region (where OCR should have recognized text there but it does not) and accepts many mis-recognized non-word symbols as text content (where OCR misreads words).

3.3 Generating XMLs From Annotated PDF Books

This process is also implemented as another JavaScript plugin menu item within Adobe Acrobat. The plugin is run on the annotated PDFs and is designed to be agnostic to the annotation types—it will work on both human-annotated and auto-annotated versions of PDFs. Once the XMLs for each children's book are generated, we could proceed to the feature extraction step. The set of features we use in the experiments are described in the following Section 4.

4 Features

For surface-level features and visual features, we utilize similar features proposed in our previous study.[3] For completeness' sake, we list these two sets of features as follows in Section 4.1:

[3] We discard two visual features in both the human and automatic annotation that require the annotation of the location of images on the page, as these were features that the Adobe Acrobat JavaScript API could not directly access.

4.1 Surface-level Features and Visually-oriented Features

- **Surface-level Features**
  1. Number of words
  2. Number of letters per word
  3. Number of sentences
  4. Average sentence length
  5. Type-token ratio of the text content.

- **Visually-oriented Features**
  1. Page count
  2. Number of words per page
  3. Number of sentences per page
  4. Number of text lines per page
  5. Number of words per text line
  6. Number of words per annotated text rectangle
  7. Number of text lines per annotated text rectangle
  8. Average ratio of annotated text rectangle area to page area
  9. Average font size

4.2 Structural Features

Since our previous work only uses surface level of text features, we are interested in investigating the contribution of high-level structural features to the current system. Feng *et al.* (2010) found several parsing-based features and part-of-speech based features to be useful. We utilize the Stanford Parser (Klein and Manning, 2003) to extract the following features from the XML files based on those used in (Feng et al., 2010):

- **Parsed Syntactic Features for NPs and VPs**
  1. Number of the NPs/VPs
  2. Number of NPs/VPs per sentence
  3. Average NP/VP length measured by number of words
  4. Number of non-terminal nodes per parse tree
  5. Number of non-terminal ancestors per word in NPs/VPs

- **POS-based Features**

1. Fraction of tokens labeled as noun/preposition
2. Fraction of types labeled as noun/preposition
3. Number of noun/preposition tokens per sentence
4. Number of noun/preposition types per sentence

5 Experiments

In the experiments, we look at how much the performance dropped by switching to zero human inputs. We also investigate the impact of using a richer set of text-based features. We apply the ranking-based book leveling algorithm proposed by our previous study (Ma et al., 2012) and use the SVM^{rank} ranker (Joachims, 2006) for our experiments. In this system, the ranker learns to sort the training books into leveled order. The unknown test book is inserted into the ordering of the training books by the trained ranking model, and the predicted reading level is calculated by averaging over the levels of the known books above and below the test book. Following the previous study, each book is uniformly partitioned into 4 parts, treating each sub-book as an individual entity. A leave-n-out procedure is utilized for evaluation: during each iteration of the training, the system leaves out all n partitions (sub-books) corresponding to one book. In the testing phase, the trained ranking model tests on all partitions corresponding to the held-out book. We obtain a single predicted reading level for the held-out book by averaging the results for all its partitions; averaging produces a more robust result. Two separate experiments are carried out on human-annotated and auto-annotated PDF books respectively.

We use two metrics to determine quality: first, the accuracy of the system is computed by claiming it is correct if the predicted book level is within ± 1 of the true reading level.[4] The second scoring metric is the absolute error of number of levels away from the key reading level, averaged over all of the books.

We report the experiment results on different combinations of feature sets: surface level features plus visually-oriented features, surface level features only, visually-oriented features only, structural features only and finally combining all the features together.

5.1 Human Annotation vs. Automatic Annotation

As we can observe from Table 3,[5] overall the human annotation gives higher accuracy than automatic annotation across different feature sets. The performance difference between human annotation and automatic annotation could be attributed to the OCR errors (described in Section 3.2) which are introduced in the automatic annotation process. However, to our surprise, the best performance of human annotation is not significantly better than automatic annotation even at $p < 0.1$ level (figures in bold).[6] Only for the experiment using all features does human annotation outperform the automatic annotation at $p < 0.1$ level (still not significantly better at $p < 0.05$ level, figures with asterisks). Therefore, we believe that the extra labor involved in the annotation step could be replaced by the automatic process without leading to a significant performance drop. While the process does still require manual scanning of each book (which can be time consuming depending on the kind of scanner), the automatic processing can reduce the labor per book from approximately twenty minutes per book to just a few seconds.

5.2 Incorporating Structural Features

Our previous study demonstrated that combining surface features with visual features produces promising results. As mentioned above, the second aim of this study is to see how much benefit we can get from incorporating high-level structural features, such as those used in (Feng et al., 2010) (described in Section 4.2), with the features in our previous study.

Table 3 shows that for both human and automatic

[4]We follow our previous study to use ± 1 accuracy evaluation metric in order to generate consistent results and allow easy comparison. Another thing to notice is that this is still rather fine-grained since multiple reading levels correspond to one single grade level.

[5]In three of the books, the OCR completely failed; thus only 94 books are available for evaluation of the automatic annotation.

[6]One-tailed Z-test was used with each book taken as an independent sample.

Annotation type	**Human**	**Automatic**
±1 *Accuracy %*		
Surface+Visual features	**76.3**	**70.2**
Surface level features	69.1	64.9
Visual features	63.9	58.5
Structural features	63.9	58.5
All features	76.3*	66.0*
Average leveling error ± standard deviation		
Surface+Visual features	0.99 ± 0.87	1.16 ± 0.83
Surface level features	1.24 ± 1.05	1.16 ± 0.97
Visual features	1.24 ± 1.00	1.37 ± 0.89
Structural features	1.30 ± 0.89	1.33 ± 0.91
All features	1.05 ± 0.78	1.15 ± 0.90

Table 3: Results on 97 books using human annotations vs. automatic annotations, reporting accuracy within one level and average error for 4 partitions per book.

annotation under the ±1 accuracy metric, the visual features and the structural features have the same performance, whose accuracy are both slightly lower than that of surface level features. By combining the surface level features with the visual features, the system obtains the best performance. However, by combining all three feature sets, the system performance does not change for human annotation whereas it hurts the performance for automatic annotation—it is likely that the OCR errors existing in the automatic annotations give rise to erroneous structural features (e.g. the parser would produce less robust parses for sentences which have out of vocabulary words). Overall, we did not observe better performance by incorporating structural features. Using structural features on their own also did not produce noteworthy results. Although among the three kinds of features (surface, visual and structural), structural features have the highest computational cost, it exhibits no significant improvement to system results. In the average leveling error metric, the best performance is again obtained at the combination of surface level features and visual features for human annotation, whereas the performance remains almost the same after incorporating structural features for automatic annotation.

6 Conclusion

In this paper, we explore the possibility of reducing human involvement in the specific task of predicting reading levels of scanned children's books by eliminating the need for human annotation. Clearly there is a trade off between the amount of human labor involved and the accuracy of the reading level predicted. Based on the experimental results, we did not observe significant performance drop by switching from human annotation to automatic annotation in the task of predicting reading levels for scanned children's books.

We also study the effect of incorporating structural features into the proposed ranking system. The experimental results showed that structural features exhibit no significant effect to the system performance. We conclude for the simply structured, short text that appears in most children's books, a deep level analysis of the text properties may be overkill for the task and produced unsatisfactory results at a high computational cost for our task.

In the future, we are interested in investigating the importance of each individual feature as well as applying various feature selection methods to further improve the overall performance of the system—in the hope that making the ranking system more robust to OCR errors introduced by automatic annotation processing. Another interesting open question is that how many scanned book pages are needed to make a good prediction.[7] Such analysis would be very helpful for practical purposes, since a teacher

[7] We thank an anonymous reviewer of the paper for this suggestion.

could just scan few sample pages instead of a full book for a reliable prediction.

References

S. Aluisio, L. Specia, C. Gasperin, and C. Scarton. 2010. Readability assessment for text simplification. In *Proceedings of the NAACL HLT 2010 Fifth Workshop on Innovative Use of NLP for Building Educational Applications*, pages 1–9. Association for Computational Linguistics.

K. Collins-Thompson and J. Callan. 2004. A language modeling approach to predicting reading difficulty. In *Proceedings of HLT / NAACL 2004*, volume 4, pages 193–200, Boston, USA.

W.H. DuBay. 2004. The principles of readability. *Impact Information*, pages 1–76.

L. Feng, M. Jansche, M. Huenerfauth, and N. Elhadad. 2010. A comparison of features for automatic readability assessment. In *Proceedings of the 23rd International Conference on Computational Linguistics (COLING 2010)*, pages 276–284, Beijing, China. Association for Computational Linguistics.

R. Flesch. 1948. A new readability yardstick. *Journal of applied psychology*, 32(3):221–233.

I. Fountas and G. Pinnell. 2010. Fountas and pinnell benchmark assessment system 1. http://www.heinemann.com/products/E02776.aspx.

M. Heilman, K. Collins-Thompson, J. Callan, and M. Eskenazi. 2007. Combining lexical and grammatical features to improve readability measures for first and second language texts. In *Proceedings of NAACL HLT*, pages 460–467.

T. Joachims. 2006. Training linear SVMs in linear time. In *Proceedings of the 12th ACM SIGKDD international conference on Knowledge discovery and data mining*, pages 217–226. ACM.

D. Klein and C. Manning. 2003. Accurate unlexicalized parsing. In *Proceedings of the 41st Meeting of the Association for Computational Linguistics*, pages 423–430.

Y. Ma, E. Fosler-Lussier, and R. Lofthus. 2012. Ranking-based readability assessment for early primary children's literature. In *Proceedings of NAACL HLT*.

S. Petersen and M. Ostendorf. 2009. A machine learning approach to reading level assessment. *Computer Speech & Language*, 23(1):89–106.

S. Schwarm and M. Ostendorf. 2005. Reading level assessment using support vector machines and statistical language models. In *Proceedings of the 43rd Annual Meeting on Association for Computational Linguistics*, pages 523–530. Association for Computational Linguistics.

L. Si and J. Callan. 2001. A statistical model for scientific readability. In *Proceedings of the tenth international conference on Information and knowledge management*, pages 574–576. ACM.

E.L. Thorndike. 1921. *The teacher's word book*, volume 134. Teachers College, Columbia University New York.

Author Index